Table of Contents

Step 1: Why Hunt Turkeys?

Step 2: Weapons for Shooting Turkeys

Step 3: Identifying Toms, Jakes and Hens

Step 4: Habitat & Food Sources

Step 5: Licensing, Hunter Safety and Rules

Step 6: Field Essentials

Step 7: Timing Your Hunt

Step 8: Scouting for Success

Step 9: Getting Permission to Hunt Private Land

Step 10: Finding Public Land to Hunt

Step 11: Arriving at your Hunting Spot

Step 12: Sun Impact

Step 13: Concealment

Step 14: Decoying

Step 15: Call Types and Sounds

Step 16: Still Hunting

Step 17: The Buddy System

Step 18: Stalking Turkeys

Step 19: Deadly Shot Placement

Step 20: You Shot a Turkey, What's Next?

Step 21: Turkey Cleaning, Preparation & Preservation

Final Words as You Start Turkey Hunting

Copyright © 2016 by GuideHunting LLC. All rights reserved.

Turkey Hunting Made Simple: A Beginners Resource to Turkey Hunting

Turkey Hunting Success is Found Right Here in this Book

In this book I teach you all of the essentials to achieve the best results possible when getting started in the sport of turkey hunting. It is my goal to save you the pain, heartache and lost time that many hunters experience in their first few seasons of hunting turkeys.

Overview:

- The first several sections of this book cover what you need to consider before you hunt such as identifying turkeys, weapons and how to find where the turkeys are.

- The second part of this book reveals the impacts of the sun, concealment techniques, and using decoys to improve success.

- The final portion of this book covers call types and sounds, shooting techniques, and what to do after you shoot a turkey.

Attention All Turkey Hunters...

"This Is A Step-By-Step Guide To Starting Turkey Hunting Hunting With No Step Missed!"

Turkey Hunting Made Simple: A Beginners Resource to Turkey Hunting

Easy to Understand Illustrations

In the book I provide several easy to understand illustrations to help you with the basic concepts of turkey hunting. These will help you quickly visualize the concepts explained in the book to be sure you understand each tactic.

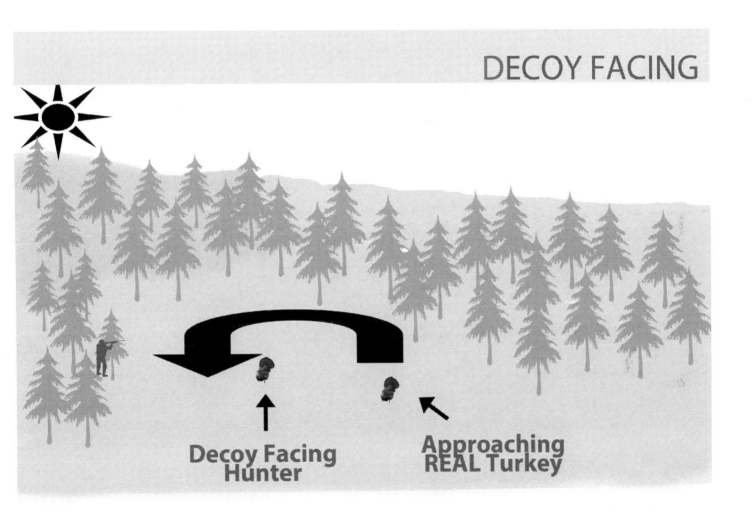

Common Mistakes Made by Turkey Hunters:

1. Not using the sun to their advantage
2. Hunting in the wrong locations
3. Incorrect shot placement

How Do You Avoid These Mistakes?

In this book I will equip you with the knowledge you need to immediately improve your success with turkey hunting. Put these lessons into action to avoid or discontinue making the common mistakes.

Who Can Benefit from This Book?

I provide relevant information for people with the following experience levels:

- People curious about turkey hunting
- People ready to start turkey hunting
- Novice turkey hunters
- Turkey hunters struggling for success

Now let's get started…

Step 1: Why Hunt Turkeys?

This Big Bird Makes for Fun Experiences

As we get started it is important to understand why you would want to hunt turkeys. There are several reasons to consider hunting turkeys including its challenges, multiple hunting methods and skills that translate to hunting other game. In this section I will cover the most common reasons people hunt turkeys and get you thinking if turkey hunting is a sport that is right for you.

Reasons to Hunt Turkeys:

- Affordable
- Excellent way to lean & teach hunting
- Relaxing
- Good for all age groups & abilities
- Great practice for other hunting
- Filler in the hunting off season
- Mild weather
- Challenging
- Taste great

Affordable

Turkey hunting is an attractive sport for many people because it is affordable to get into. This is in contrast to many other types of hunting such as big game or waterfowl hunting where the costs of all of the gear needed could easily be several thousand dollars or more. Sure, with turkey hunting there is some nice to have equipment and that could add to the cost but to get started all you really need is a hunting license, camouflage, a turkey decoy, a shotgun and a box of shells. Chances are you may own a shotgun or be able to borrow one from a friend or relative so for less than $100 total you should be able to try this sport out and see if it is something that you enjoy. Once you realize you enjoy the sport you can always add to your hunting gear as your budget allows.

Excellent Way to Learn & Teach Hunting

Another great thing about turkey hunting is that it is a good way to learn and teach hunting skills. I am not saying that turkey hunting is easy but it does provide for good learning opportunities. For beginning hunters the skills you can learn with turkey hunting are transferrable to other types of hunting, especially big game hunting. The skills include shooting moving game, proper concealment, decoying and stalking. This means that you can use the trial and error that happens when you turkeys for hunting other elusive species.

Relaxing

Many forms of hunting require a lot of work. Consider duck hunting where you may be setting up dozens of decoys and trudging through the water to retrieve downed ducks. When you utilize the still hunting method for turkey hunting it can require a very minimal amount of physical exertion. You simply get to your hunting spot and sit and wait. This is in contrast to some types of game hunting where you must walk long distances to keep up with your game. For example, elk hunting often requires trekking through treacherous land to stalk elk and get within shooting distance.

Good for All Age Groups & Abilities

Pretty much all age groups can partake in this enjoyable activity. Both older hunters and physically disabled hunters may not able to navigate difficult terrain often encountered during waterfowl hunting, big game hunting or even small game hunting. This makes the sport of turkey hunting a good option for them. The ability to simply hunt on the side of a field while sitting on a chair and concealed by a blind should lend itself for nearly every age, skill level and physical ability to enjoy this outdoor activity.

Great Practice for Other Hunting

Another excellent reason for hunting turkeys is it can provide practice for hunting other birds. To hunt turkeys you need to use similar strategies for big game and waterfowl hunting such as decoying, shooting game in movement, camouflage and blind concealment. If you are a beginning hunter there are not many other ways to get quality practice to implement in all kinds of hunting. Even for experienced hunters, shooting turkeys will hone your shooting skills so you can be as prepared as possible for your next waterfowl or big game hunting trip.

Not only will turkey hunting provide practice for waterfowl and big game hunting but it also provides practice for other small game such as squirrels, chipmunks and gophers. Turkeys regularly sit on the branches of trees for roosting, travel through heavily wooded areas and run quickly on the ground. All of these scenarios are situations that you can encounter with small game hunting. Hunting these challenging turkeys allow you to improve your shooting in these situations while providing a fun experience all at once.

Great Filler in the Hunting Offseason
Another benefit of turkey hunting is that the season is open during many days that other game hunting seasons are closed. As an example, I hunt for ducks and the season for ducks usually starts the last week of September and goes until early December in my area. However, turkey season often occurs in both the spring and fall. This means that you could hunt during the spring as well as a few additional weeks in early fall before many other hunting seasons open up. This can be a great way to get outdoors and hunting while you wait for other hunting seasons to open. Additionally, a few weeks of practice hunting the challenging turkeys prior to other hunting never hurt.

Mild Weather
Turkey hunting is also attractive to hunters because the mild weather that is experienced during the turkey hunting season. In many states the season is in the spring and early fall. For example early season months may be April and May and the fall months might be October and November. Throughout a vast majority of the states these months will have warm to mild temperatures that can make it quite enjoyable to sit outside for a morning or afternoon of turkey hunting. Even in the states that experience cold winters, early November is often still not horribly cold. This means that even to the end of the turkey season the outside temperatures should provide for an enjoyable outdoor experience without freezing your tail off.

Challenging
Once you begin hunting turkeys you will realize that this can be a challenging sport but its challenges can make for great enjoyment. To be successful with turkey hunting you need to understand turkey behavior, concealment, decoying and proper shooting techniques. Unlike

some game hunting such as squirrel, dove and waterfowl hunting, the success rates are typically lower for each time you get out hunting. However, this makes the sport fun because it is not a sport that you typically just happen upon having success so when you are successful it is satisfying because that you were able to fool these intelligent and elusive birds.

Taste Great

A final reason is that turkeys can have a great flavor. Unlike some game animals such as squirrels, chipmunks, geese and even ducks a lot of people find the flavor of turkeys to be quite tasty. So with turkey hunting not only can this be a fun outdoors activity but it can also produce some very tasty and unique meals that you could share with friends and family. It can be a great conversation piece when you prepare turkeys for visitors.

Now let's examine weapon options for turkey hunting …

Step 2: Weapons for Shooting Turkeys

Select from a Variety of Guns for Hunting Turkeys

A great aspect that keeps turkey hunting interesting is the wide range of weapons you can choose from. Each type of weapon has its own unique strengths and challenges for hunting turkeys. To mix up your turkey hunting you can try mastering one of these weapons and then move onto another one to experience the satisfaction in bagging turkeys regardless of the weapon you select.

The good news is that most of the weapons for turkey hunting are relatively affordable. The least expensive of the weapons used for turkey hunting can be purchased for around $200 brand new. Of course you could spend a lot more money if you go with high-end brands and get extra features, but to get started and to see if you enjoy the sport there is absolutely no need to let the cost of the weapons prohibit you from turkey hunting.

Most common weapons for turkey hunting:

- Shotguns
- Bows

Shotguns

Using a shotgun is a very effective way to hunt turkeys that are in close range and even on the run. The reason is that a shotgun disperses multiple BBs each time you pull the trigger making a large killing area. Particularly when turkeys are on the run the shotgun is going to be your best option as long as they are close enough to hit. Keep in mind that shotguns typically have an effective range of about 40 yards so you need to plan your shots to be within 40 yards. There are some extended range choke tubes that you can buy and some ammunition available claims to have further killing ranges but in most cases you really should plan to be within 40 yards of the turkey before shooting.

If you are not familiar with choke tubes they are a few inch metal tube that fits in the end of your shotgun barrel and changes the tightness of the pattern of the BBs coming out of your gun. Some choke tubes make the disbursement of your BBs wide while other tubes condense the pattern. The tubes for turkey hunting are typically designed to make your patterns tighter and that can help increase the range of your BBs. When looking to buy a choke tube the packaging will clearly list what the intended outcome of BB distribution is when using it.

Even with a shotgun it will be challenging to hit a turkey on the run. Not only are they fast, but they quickly change direction when they are running and the areas where you will find turkeys can often have many obstructions such as brush or trees in the way. If you are someone who is going to be relying on turkey meat as a food source, then a shotgun is a great option. However, if you want to increase the difficulty level of shooting a turkey, then you could consider a bow which I will discuss in a minute.

As far as shotguns, there are two different types to select from. There are semi-automatic and pump shotguns. Semi-automatic shotguns automatically load in the next shell after you shoot so you can take successive shots quickly. However, the downside of a semi-automatic shotgun is the cost. These guns usually start around $700. If you are going to be doing other types of hunting such as waterfowl hunting the extra cost to invest in the semi-automatic shotgun might be well worth it. I have had a semi-automatic shotgun for several years and truly enjoy the ease with which you can fire multiple rounds.

The other type of shotgun is a pump shotgun. With this shotgun type you must use the pump mechanism to load in the next round each time after you shoot. Although there is an increase in time between shots compared to the semi-automatic shotgun, pump shotguns can be very effective and with some practice you will be able to reload shells quickly. The best part is that pump shotguns are less expensive than semi-automatic shotguns and start around $300 brand new.

You also need to select a gauge of shotgun to buy. When considering what gauge shotgun you should get, I would recommend a 12-gauge for turkey hunting. For chamber size I would recommend a 3-inch chamber. Most shell lengths you will use for turkey are 2 ¾-inch and 3 inch so a 3 inch chamber should work fine. However, you could consider getting a 3 ½ inch chamber which gives you some flexibility if you decide to go with a larger shell but usually 3 ½ inch chambers are more expensive so it is not totally necessary. Regarding the barrel length, a 26-inch barrel would work well. This is because it will keep the shot pattern tight enough but it won't be too long for those times when you are walking around in the woods. You could go up to a 28-inch barrel, but it would just be a little more difficult to maneuver in thick brush and trees.

Regardless of the size of ammunition you choose it is very important that you pattern your shotgun before you bring it turkey hunting. Basically, patterning a shotgun means shooting it at targets of varying distances to see how the BBs hit the target and what the distribution of BBs looks like on the target. As an example you could setup targets at 20, 40,60 and 80 yards and see what the targets look like after you shoot. Examining the targets should give you a good idea on how effective the shotgun will be at each range and the killing radius that the shots will have at each distance. It is important to do this with your gun because you can read the box of shotgun shells and choke tubes on what their recommend ranges are but each shotgun will perform slightly differently. You should take the time do to this before you head out hunting to avoid missing turkeys that you thought you should be able to kill from a certain distance.

Bows

For hunters who are looking to add an additional level of challenge to turkey hunting you could consider hunting with a bow. Bow hunting has been around for ages and used for taking a variety of game animals. As of recently, bows have become popular for turkey hunting. Part of this increase in popularity for the use of bows in turkey hunting is the increase of people using bows for hunting big game so now that more people already have a bow it is exciting to use it for other hunting.

Your range for shooting turkeys with a bow is going to be significantly less than a shotgun. For the highest probability shots with a bow you should plan on being within about 15-30 yards of the turkey. Due to how close you have to be in order to shoot a turkey with a bow it can really make for an exciting but challenging experience.

A few other challenges to mention about using a bow is the learning curve. Learning to use a bow and learning to shoot at distances accurately will typically take someone much longer than it would with a shotgun or rifle. People often practice months or even years before they get to be average at shooting effectively with a bow. In contrast most people could learn to shoot a gun well enough to hit a still animal with just a few hours or a few days of practice.

However, after pointing out the downsides of bow hunting I do not want you to be discouraged with the thought of using them for turkey hunting. As I have already mentioned it can be a thrilling experience to hunt with bows because you are going to be much closer to the turkeys for shooting and that can be exciting. In addition, many people like bow hunting because of the personal satisfaction that they get from using this more challenging way of hunting versus a shotgun. Shotguns are great weapons but you really do have a significant advantage over the game you hunt with them because of some of the killing distances you can achieve as well as the killing radius they have. Using a bow levels the playing field with turkeys and thus increasing personal satisfaction when you successfully bag a turkey.

Now let's examine how to identify different turkeys…

Step 3: Identifying Toms, Jakes and Hens

Learn to Identify Turkeys Before Hunting

It is extremely important to know how to identify turkeys so you shoot the correct gender and not make a mistake of shooting the wrong bird. Identifying turkeys will come easier as you hunt more often, but this will give you a brief overview of how to identify turkeys. The good news is that with really only three variations of turkeys to identify you should be able to identify them quickly with just a little bit of practice.

Turkey Hunting Made Simple: A Beginners Resource to Turkey Hunting

IDENTIFYING TURKEYS

Tom　　　　　　　　　Jake　　　　　　　　　Hen

Toms, Jakes & Hens

Telling the difference between turkeys as you get start may feel intimidating but in this section I will help outline some of the easiest ways to identify Turkeys. We will be looking at the three variations of turkeys which are toms, jakes and hens. The tom turkeys are the adult male turkeys and are the turkeys that are sought after by most turkey hunters. Jakes are males but are not full grown like toms and the hens are the female turkeys. You can typically shoot tom or jake turkeys and in some cases you may be able to shoot hens.

- Color
- Size
- Feathers
- Beard

- Spurs

Color

The first big difference between the types of turkeys will be their color. Toms and jakes tend to have the darkest feathers and in many cases the feathers are nearly black or at least a dark charcoal gray. The hens will be somewhat lighter in color with tan or brown ends to their wings. In addition, toms and jakes will have red or blue heads or a combination of both while the hens will have a gray or brown head.

Size

Another big difference between the variations of turkeys is the size of the birds. The toms are by far the largest and can get up to 20 pounds or even a little bit larger than that. The size of the jakes will typically be smaller than the toms because they are still maturing and working their way up to the size of a Tom. Hens are smaller than the toms, approximately half the size, weighting in at 6-12 pounds.

Feathers

One of the quickest ways to identify the differences in the birds are the feathers, particularly the tail feathers. Both the toms and jakes have long tail feathers that can be spread out into a fan look to attract a mate while the hens lack these large tail feathers. In addition, the easiest way to tell the difference between a tom and a jake is the spread of the tail feathers. As illustrated in the picture from this section the toms tail feathers fan out into a nice rounded half moon shape. The jakes tail feathers also fan out but you will notice that the middle tail feathers are a few inches longer than the rest of the tail feathers and the difference is quite noticeable.

Beard

A beard is a bunch of long black hairs that come out of front of the chest area of turkeys. These hairs are several inches long and the hair is course and stiff. Typically beards are seen on the toms and you can see the beard clearly on the tom in the picture in this section. However, often jakes will have beards and rarely are beards found on hens but it can happen about 10% of the time.

Spurs

The spurs on turkeys are like claws that are located on the back sides of the legs and are used for battling with other turkeys and protection. Turkey spurs are found on the tom and jake turkeys and vary rarely on the hens. Typically the longer the spur length the older the Turkey is. The male turkeys use their spurs to fight with other turkeys that are on their territory or to fight off male turkeys from hens that they want to mate with.

Now let's learn about turkey habitat...

Step 4: Habitat & Food Sources

What Do Turkeys Eat and Where do They Live?

When hunting any species it is useful to know what they eat and where the species are found. Knowing what turkeys commonly eat can help you figure out the prime hunting locations because if you setup near where turkeys eat then you are likely to have success. Additionally, you must know if turkeys are located in your area to be able to hunt them. In this section I will cover some of the most common types of food that turkeys eat and where you can often find turkeys.

Where Turkeys Are Found?

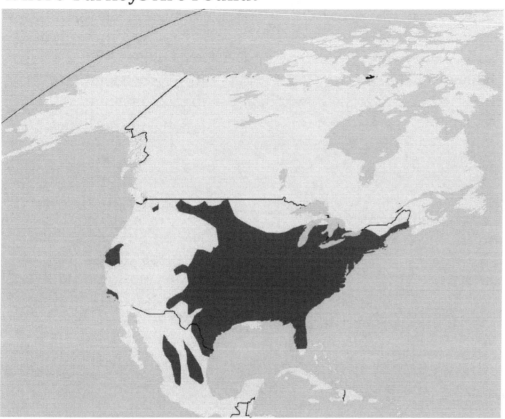

Wild turkeys are found throughout a good portion of the United States, but primarily throughout the middle to eastern states. There is also a population of turkeys along the west cost including California and some sub species are found in Mexico as well. This is great news for those who want to try out the sport because regardless of where you live in the United States you should be within a reasonable distance to find some turkeys if you are willing to put in some windshield time.

Where Do Turkeys Hang Out?

Now that we know that you can find turkeys in a good portion of the continental United States, let's take a look at where you are likely to find turkeys hanging out. These are some of ideas on where to start to find the turkeys but of course there are more areas as well. As you hunt more in your area you will start to see what areas the turkeys are located at most often.

The Roost

The ideal place you want to hunt near is the roost of the turkeys. The roost will be the tree that the turkeys go into at night to sleep. These will usually be larger trees that have branches large enough to support the weight of several turkeys. As you scout areas near sundown or just before sunrise you will want to pay particular attention to the trees. Turkeys should be pretty easy to spot as there would be many large black spots in the tree. If you find the roost you should be at a great advantage to have success hunting turkeys.

Near Food

In addition to finding the roost, you can also put yourself in a position near where turkeys are going to feed. In the next section I'm going to cover some of the most common items that turkeys like to eat so you will have a good handle on their food preferences. Like any bird, turkeys need to eat so it only makes sense to find them near their source of food. You will find that turkeys in your area may prefer one food source over another or perhaps you live in a part of the country where one food source is more abundant than others. For example, turkeys enjoy eating nuts so if you happen to live in an area where there are a lot of walnut trees you can likely expect to find some turkeys there.

What Do Turkeys Eat?
- Sunflower seeds
- Corn
- Berries
- Roots
- Fruits
- Walnuts
- Vegetables
- Acorns
- Hickory
- Pine
- Clover
- Field grass
- Worms
- Insects

Near Water

All animals need to drink water at some point which means that setting up near water is likely in a spot where you will eventually see some turkeys. Ponds, rivers, lakes and streams are some areas where it will be common to find turkeys drinking and roosting. This makes hunting locations that are in between tree lines and water sources a great place to setup shop for turkey hunting.

Woods

Another favorite spot for turkeys to roost is the tree lines that border fields. Turkeys roost in trees as the tree line provides them elevation to see predators but the tree line also provides concealment from strong winds while they rest. They also like these areas because they are within quick access to open flying spots.

Open Areas

In addition to woods, turkeys also like to hang out in open areas. This includes fields, prairies, and grassy areas just to name a few. As an example, a copped down cornfield is a prime spot to find turkeys. This open area allows the turkeys plenty of sight distance to watch out for any potential predators. Also, the cut down corn stalks creates for easy feeding by the turkeys as they can simply pick away at corn kernels and husks left behind during harvest. Find yourself a concealed area on the side of a harvested field and you should be in for some pretty good turkey hunting.

Near Barns and Farm Buildings

For those of you who will be hunting on private property such as farms a great place to find turkeys is near barns and farm buildings. Areas near barns are likely to have some type of food nearby. For example, there might be grain or corn that the farmer is using to feed his cattle and as he brings it to the cattle there is a possibility that some of the food could fall out onto the open ground. This can make for a quick and easy meal for the turkeys.

However, one downside about finding turkeys near barns and farm buildings is the obstruction that these areas can cause when shooting turkeys. There is often more than one building located nearby when hunting a farm so you have to be conscious of this if you are planning to hunt turkeys near farm buildings. It is best to plan out your clear shooting lanes when you approach these areas so that you know in advance of exactly where you can safely shoot and areas that you need to avoid. In addition, many hunting regulations call that you must be a certain distance from any buildings to discharge a firearm. Just be sure to check your local regulations before hunting near buildings to ensure you are compliant with all regulations.

Now let's find out how to be safe and follow the rules when turkey hunting...

Step 5: Licensing, Hunter Safety and Rules

Make Sure you Have the Proper Licenses and Any Applicable Safety Registration

It is important to make sure you have the proper licensing and learn hunting safety prior to heading out for a turkey hunting adventure. The laws and regulations for turkey hunting are very different from one area to the next. This means that you will want to check your states regulations to ensure that you are fully compliant with applicable laws. Additionally, you may need to have some type of safety certification to hunt turkeys which is in addition to the license you need to harvest a turkey.

Legal aspects to consider before hunting:

- Area you are hunting
- Specific hunting dates
- Toms, jakes & hens
- Safety certification
- Hunting rules

Area

When you are going to purchase your hunting license, the first thing you will need to know is what area you plan to hunt. In some states, the turkey hunting licenses are good for the entire state that you purchase the license in, but if you will be hunting in multiple states then you will probably need multiple licenses. Be aware that if you are not a resident of the state you plan to hunt in you will typically pay a higher rate for your license. Sometimes it can be as much as double what it costs for a resident of that state to buy a license. However, in some states there are different zones which are sections of the state that are predetermined by the wildlife office. Certain zones may have different hunting restrictions.

You should also consider what other type of hunting or fishing you plan to do within that year before you buy a hunting license. Some states allow you to purchase a combination license that will give you hunting and fishing privileges for a slightly discounted rate. Not only do you save a little money this way but it also helps reduce the amount of paperwork you need to carry with you.

Hunting Dates

In addition to knowing what areas you plan to hunt turkeys, you will also need to know the dates you plan to hunt them. For example a state may have 5 different spring turkey hunting seasons. Each season may run only 1 or 2 weeks long and when you buy a license it is only good for one of those seasons.

Toms, Jakes & Hens

As I mentioned earlier there are Tom, Jake and Hen turkeys. When it comes to actually hunting turkeys there are often rules on what type of turkey you can shoot. In some areas you will only be allowed to shoot a tom turkey. In some areas you may only be able to shoot a male turkey and some areas may not have any restrictions on what type of turkey you shoot even if it is a hen. Also, sometimes you can only shoot bearded turkeys during certain times of the year such as the spring. As I mentioned mostly Toms and Jakes will have beards but occasionally a hen may have a beard as well.

Just be sure you understand the regulations and that you properly identify the turkey before you bull the trigger. Unfortunately, not knowing the rules is not a valid excuse if a game warden catches you without proper licensing or with a type of turkey you are not allowed to shoot. The penalties can be very harsh for people who violate the rules including loss of hunting privileges and confiscation of hunting equipment.

Safety Certification

In addition to having proper licensing, you will also need to ensure that you obtain any necessary safety certifications prior to hunting turkeys. Again, the rules in each area are different. In some areas you will need to have a formal safety certification regardless of your age. In other areas if you are over a certain age you do not need to have safety training.

Even if your area does not require any safety training, it is an excellent idea to go through a safety training course prior to doing any type of hunting. Although hunting can be a very fun activity, it also comes with a certain level of safety risk. You can never eliminate all safety risks when hunting, but going through a formal safety class will teach you skills to improve your safety practices. Hunting safety courses often range from $20 to $100 for a course that will last a few weeks. This is a great investment in your long-term safety.

Bag Limits

Some areas have season limits on the number of turkeys you can kill and have in your possession so make sure you know these rules before going out. In many areas you can only shoot one turkey per season but then again there are other areas where turkey populations are high and you can harvest more than one Turkey. Also, some areas may allow you to shoot one turkey with a bow and one with a gun. Again, always check your regulations to ensure you know how many turkeys you are allowed to shoot before you head out for a turkey hunt.

Now let's take a look at useful tools for turkey hunting…

Step 6: Field Essentials

Bring these Items to Prepare for Hunting Turkeys

Now that we have discussed weapon types and shells, let's take a look at some of the other items that you may want to bring with you on your hunting trip. I am going to cover the major items in this section but there may be other items you want to bring after you hunt some and realize what you prefer to have with in the field. These items should give you a good start on what to have with for a fun and successful turkey hunting trip.

What else should I bring with hunting?

- Clothing
- Face Paint/Face Mask
- Hunting blind
- Chair
- Shooting stick
- Hunting knife
- Binoculars

- Bug spray
- Toilet paper
- Compass
- Food & water

Clothing

One primary key to hunting turkeys is remaining well concealed from their sight. Turkeys have extremely good eyesight so it is extremely important to ensure that you are well camouflaged, from head to toe, to ensure that you are not spotted by wild turkeys. You will need a camouflage shirt, pants, hat and gloves. Even if it is warm outside during the time that you are hunting you will still want to have at least lightweight gloves on because they will cover your skin from the sight of nearby turkeys.

Face Paint/Face Mask

In addition to camouflage clothing, another method you can use to take concealment to a higher level is utilizing face paint. Depending on how well you are concealed from the turkeys it is possible that the turkeys could see the skin on your face and be scared off. A simple solution to this is to buy a few tubes of camo face paint and apply it prior to turkey hunting. A tube of face paint should be around $5-10 and it should be plenty of face paint for several hunting trips. This is not an absolute must but if you really want to try and reduce your chances of being spotted by Turkeys then this is an option.

Hunting Blind

Another tool that you will want to consider utilizing when hunting for turkeys is a hunting blind. There are several different styles of hunting blinds that you can chose from but the basic purpose of a hunting blind is to conceal yourself form the direct sight of turkeys. Some hunting blinds are as simple as a roll of mesh camouflage material that you can stake out in front of you while you sit on the ground. Other hunting blinds are essentially small camouflage tents that have window openings that you can shoot through at the approaching turkeys. Not only do blinds conceal your body but they also conceal movement. For example, if you are bow hunting you will need to draw your bow back prior to shooting. With a hunting blind you will be able to use the covering to reduce the chances of the turkeys seeing you move as you prepare to shoot.

Chair

There are several chairs that you can use for turkey hunting including specifically designed hunting chairs, lawn chairs and folding chairs. Essentially most hunting chairs that you buy are camouflage versions of a lawn chair. If you are looking to get started with turkey hunting on a budget there is really no need to go out and buy a fancy hunting chair to start. Simply grab an extra lawn chair or folding chair and bring that with you to the field. As long as you have the chair properly concealed inside of a blind the existing chairs you already own will work just fine. Actually, if you do not want to go and buy a chair you could even use a 5 gallon bucket to sit on. However, if you are not going to be using a hunting blind then you will need to ensure that you get a camouflage chair so it is not spotted by turkeys.

Another option for sitting on is a padded seat cushion. If you go to any sporting goods store they should have these cushions in camouflage or black. They will be very inexpensive running around $10 which makes it a great investment if you will be hunting from the ground. These cushions are great for those times that you will be be actively walking for turkeys because they are lightweight and when you decide to sit for a few minutes they allow you much more comfort compared to sitting on the hard ground.

Shooting Stick

One hunting accessory you may want to consider particularly for still hunting turkeys is a shooting stick. Basically a shooting stick is a plastic rod that has a "V" on the top end of the rod where you place your gun. This allows you to set the gun on the top and stabilize it while you wait for the perfect shot on the approaching turkey. There may be times where it takes quite a while for the turkey to get into the spot where you want to take your shot. Without a shooting stick you may end up raising and lowing your gun multiple times as your arms get tired. This added movement can increase the chances of you being spotted by the turkey and completely missing out on the opportunity to shoot the bird.

Hunting Knife

A hunting knife is an important tool that you will want to bring with on your Turkey hunting adventure. After you shoot a turkey you will need a knife to be able to clean it to remove the meat. Make sure that you sharpen your knife before you go hunting because a sharp knife makes cutting easier. Surprisingly a sharp knife adds to your safety because you won't have to push so hard to cut which will reduce the chances of the knife slipping and you cutting yourself.

Binoculars

Investing in a set of binoculars for hunting is an excellent way check out your surroundings. The great thing is you do not need to spend a significant amount of money to get yourself a pair of binoculars to increase your viewing distance. For several years I used a set of binoculars that I purchased for $20. Sure there are more expensive pairs you can buy but even the cheap binoculars can greatly improve your viewing distance.

One of the most useful times to utilize binoculars for turkey hunting is when you are hunting on the side of an open field. With binoculars you can see to the other side of the field and the edges of the fields on the other side as well as checking treelines. They will help you be able to identify what kind of turkey is approaching well in advance of the turkey coming within shooting distance. You will also find binoculars useful as you scout for turkeys. When driving around you are able to look out the window and check for turkeys in fields, on the ground and look for turkeys roosting in trees.

Bug Spray

When sitting on the side of a field waiting for turkeys to come nearby there is a chance that there may be mosquitos, wood ticks and other bugs in the area. You will notice heavy bugs in the early morning and late afternoon. This could be even more common depending on the time of season that you hunt. Many turkey hunting seasons open up in the early fall so it is likely that mosquitoes and bugs will still be active in these warmer temperatures. Even if you do not put any bug spreay on prior to heading out your turkey hunting trip it can be a great idea to throw a can of it in your backpack of gear. This way you can avoid spending the entire day fending off bugs.

Toilet Paper

Honestly it is a great idea to bring a roll of toilet paper with in your hunting backpack. If you plan on having a several hour turkey hunt then there is a chance that you will have to use the restroom at some point. The good news is that the outdoors will provide many areas where you can use the restroom in a concealed spot. Unfortunately, if you do not bring toilet paper and nature calls you may find it necessary to cut your hunt short and head out for a restroom. Do yourself a favor and throw a roll of toilet paper in a ziplock bag and put it in your backpack in case of emergency. Storing the toilet paper inside of a ziplock bag ensures that it will remain dry.

Compass

Depending on the location you are going to hunt and how familiar you are with the area you are in, it can be a great idea to bring a compass with you. Any time that you are hunting a new area you should bring a compass for safety. The chances of getting lost are pretty slim but it is better to have one with you just to be safe.   Especially if you are going to hunt on public land that you have not hunted before it would be a good idea to bring a compass. If you have a compass app on your phone that would work great so you don't have to carry an additional item with you. However the downside is many compass apps require reception so if you are in a remote area without reception they will be useless. The other risk is if your phone runs out of batteries you will now be without a compass.

Food & Water

I do recommend bringing some water and food with on your hunting trip. When you are going to hunt for just an hour or so a bottle of water and a snack bar should get you through. Having just this little bit of food and water can help keep you hydrated and energized. When you plan longer trips you may want to bring a few bottles of water and even pack a lunch. Without food and water you might have to stop hunting sooner than you want. With some food and water you can extend your hunting trip, particularly on those days when you are having good success.

Now let's find out when to hunt...

Step 7: Timing Your Hunt

Enjoy the Opportunities Created By Each Season

Each time of year does have its benefits but each time of year can also present some challenges. Let's take a look at the different seasons for turkey hunting and what each provides for hunting excitement. Keep in mind this is a generic description of the season and can vary from region to region.

Seasons:

- Spring
- Fall

Time:

- Morning
- Mid-day
- Sunset

Spring

The spring is the prime time for turkey hunting because it is breeding season. Male turkeys will be actively seeking mates so if you can reproduce a scene with a female turkey there is a good chance that you will have some good hunting. This peak time where the males are wanting to mate is called the "rut". Since the males will be eager to mate they will become more aggressive and even more territorial. They will want to fend off intruders so putting a tom or jake turkey decoy out during this time of year may work well in getting a large tom to come to you looking for a fight.

In addition, in the spring of the year you are going to be hunting turkeys who have been dealing with harsh temperatures and weather for the last several months of winter so this means that they will be likely to be a little more active during this time. The turkeys are looking forward to some easier to find meals than what they likely had during the winter. These factors makes the springtime one of the best times to hunt turkeys.

Vegetation is starting to grow back during this time but it is likely that plants and crops might not yet be at the point where their height will hinder your ability to see turkeys as they come out into the open. This is great because you can take advantage of some of the higher spots such as hillsides that turkeys may head to as they search for their next meal. When they head to the higher spots you should be able to see the turkeys much easier and be able to place a clear shot without any obstruction.

Fall

As the year progresses into the fall it becomes easier to see turkeys in the woods and fields. In many areas late September and going into October the leaves will be falling off the trees and the shrubs and brush on the ground will thin out which will help create better visibility. This makes the fall another great time of year to shoot turkeys. Additionally you benefit because the temperatures are a little cooler compared to the summer but probably not cold enough to be uncomfortable yet.

One piece of information regarding the seasons for turkey hunting is that the turkeys may pattern differently in the spring compared to the fall. In most areas that have turkey hunting seasons there is a spring and fall season but be aware that how the turkeys behave can be different. You might notice significantly different locations where the turkeys move through. For example, if you had good success in a specific location in the spring for turkey hunting that same area might not be good for the fall. After several months the turkeys can change their daily patterns so it will likely be necessary to scout locations again in the fall before heading out for a hunt. Just do not assume the turkeys will be in the same spot from one hunting season to the next.

Morning

The first few hours of sunlight can be some of the absolute best times to hunt turkeys. Like many other birds and animals, turkeys head out for their first meal of the day shortly after sunrise. They have gone the entire evening without eating so now they should be hungry and will head to their food source. This is a great time to get within trails trails to their feeding grounds so find fields with abundant food sources, particularly seeds and nuts, and get ready for action. In addition, they will also often drink within the first few hours and as I mentioned earlier, turkeys often roost in trees near sources of water. This means that setting up in between trees and the nearby water sources can be a great morning hunting spot. All of these reasons that make turkeys active in the first few hours of the morning a great reason to hunt turkeys in the morning.

Mid-Day

After the first peak hunting hours of the morning the activity of turkeys typically slows down during the midday. Depending on where you will be hunting the hours will vary but this could typically be the hours of approximately 11am to around 4pm. During the midday the turkeys tend to be less active and rest during these times. However, I do not want you to get discouraged from heading out for a turkey hunt in the midday. Even though the active turkey numbers may dip during this time, if you have scouted your location well and setup on a active turkey path you can be in for some good midday hunts.

To be successful in the midday you want to be where the turkeys are. Most turkeys have probably had their first meal of the day by now but may still be looking for something to drink or even searching for a mate. Try finding ridgelines where turkeys have trails through the woods and setup on a spot that is within shooting distance. As the turkeys walk along these paths you should be in good shooting position.

Sunset

The last few hours of sunlight provide excellent shooting opportunities, similar to the first few hours of the day. The behaviors that turkeys had in the morning will typically be repeated by doves before it gets dark outside. The turkeys want to fill up their bellies in preparation of being in their roost during the evening hours. This means that the turkeys will be back out to feed and quite often they will return to the same feeding spots that they visited during the morning.

A key to successful turkey hunting is scouting, here are some tips...

Step 8: Scouting for Success

How to Select the Proper Location to Hunt Turkeys

As with most hunting the more time you invest finding the spots where your game is located the higher the chances are that you will be successful when you head out for the actual hunt. This holds true with turkey hunting as well. Let's take a look at some good places to go turkey hunting.

Identifying Areas for Turkey Hunting:

- Pay attention to where you see turkeys
- Call for turkeys when scouting
- Prairies and fields
- Woods
- Near water
- Use trail cameras
- Look for tracks
- Observe for droppings

Pay Attention to Where you See Turkeys

This should be obvious but you want to pay attention to where you see turkeys. When you are driving around keep an eye out in the fields and woods and actively look for turkeys. If you often see turkeys in a certain area this should be a great place for you to start. Also, you can ask your friends and family to be on the lookout for you. Let them know that you want to go turkey hunting and ask if they could pay attention to what they are seeing. It is better to have several people searching for turkeys rather than doing it alone and often time's friends and family will be willing to help you out with this.

Another strategy to get the feedback of others on good places to hunt is to make a posting to your favorite social media website and let people know that you are looking to go turkey hunting. Ask and see if your friends have suggestions on where to go. This is a great way to get the word out to a lot of people at once and often time's people will be willing to help you out and provide some ideas. If people do not know that you want to hunt turkeys there is no way your friend can help you out. You may be pleasantly surprised on the success you have in finding a spot for turkey hunting when you simply ask for help.

Call for Turkeys When Scouting

When you are out driving around looking for a hunting spot I would recommend that you bring your turkey calls with you. Although you are not planning on hunting that day you can use this as an opportunity to test your calling and see if you get any responses from turkeys in the area. Step out of your vehicle and start calling. Do this for a good 5- 10 minutes to see if you can get any response from nearby turkeys. If you are able to get a response in this short period of time you have likely found a hunting spot that is worth coming back to when it is actually time for your hunting trip.

Prairies and Fields

Open prairies and fields are some of the absolute best places to hunt for turkeys. These open areas are excellent hunting grounds as the turkeys can see long distances and be aware of any predators as well as search for easily accessible food. This in turn makes for good hunting spots because as the turkeys are out searching for their food you can be out searching for the turkeys. In addition, prairies and fields are good for hunting because you usually have great viewing distances to spot those turkeys. Try and find the higher spots and tree lines to sit near because they will give you increased viewing distance as turkeys come out of hiding while keeping you concealed from their sight.

Woods

Although woods are a good place to find turkeys, woods are also a challenging place to shoot turkeys. The trees, branches and leaves can make it challenging to see turkeys in this type of environment. Once a turkey starts running in the woods you will have minimal time to be able to shoot it. They run very fast and the further away they get from you the more branches and leaves that will be in your shooting lane to the turkey.

When hunting in the woods it is best to try and find an area that has somewhat of a clearing. This will allow you to have a little more of an opportunity to shoot at the turkeys without much in the way. Areas where you hunt for turkeys are often the same areas where people hunt for deer or other wild game. The great thing about hunting in an area that is used for deer hunting is that there are likely going to be some deer hunting stands that you could use to sit in for hunting turkeys. Anytime you can get to a high spot you are put at an advantage as you can see longer distances. In addition, by being elevated up in the air you are put out of the direct line of sight of the turkeys.

Near Water

For turkeys you will often find their roost relatively near a water source. The roost is the trees that turkeys sit in to to sleep for the night. A great place to check for turkeys is in tree lines that border ponds, rivers and lakes. Another reason why hunting near water is good is because all animals need to drink water at some point so it is likely you will eventually see some turkeys. In the late fall season during very cold days any open water spots can be a prime spot for hunting because as most water has frozen over the few spots that are open and easily accessible are going to be highly frequented by turkeys.

Use Trail Cameras

A fun way to validate that there are turkeys in the area you plan to hunt is to utilize trail cameras. Basically a trail camera is a camera that you can attach to a tree, fencepost or other stationary item in a high traffic area. Then the camera captures pictures when there is motion anywhere in the area. You can affix the trail camera by wrapping straps around the tree at a height that will pick up the image you are trying to get, for turkeys this would be about 3-4 feet off the ground.

Trail camera technology has come a long way and it is truly amazing what you can do with them now. Many trail cameras operate with a memory card system where you plug in a memory card and any pictures that are taken are stored on the card. You can then view these images on a computer or even some mobile phones can pull images from the memory card. In the recent years there have started to be some trail cameras that work with an internet connection so any images taken by the camera are sent directly to your mobile phone for instant viewing. This is really great because it saves you the time and money of driving to your hunting spot several times to check the memory card. However, the downside is the trail cameras with this feature are significantly more expensive than the standard memory card style.

Look for Tracks

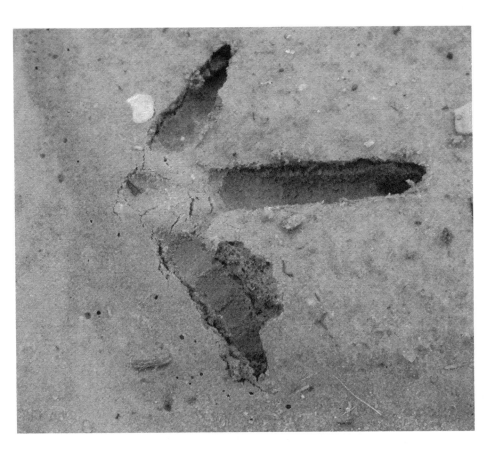

Another sure fire way to know if there are turkeys in the area are to look for turkey tracks left on the ground. However, you will likely not see these unless there is soft ground, mud or snow on the ground. Hunting for turkeys in the snow or after a recent rainfall when the ground is soft will be some of the best times to be able to see where turkeys are traveling from the footprints they leave.

The prints consist of three long fingers with the longest finger pointing in the direction that the turkey was walking and two other fingers at and angle on each side of the main finger. The nice thing about turkey tracks is they look very distinct compared to other animals. For example, animals with paws can be much more difficult to determine what type of animal was there where even novice turkey hunters should be able to easily identify a turkey track.

Observe for Droppings

Another indicator of turkeys in the area is their droppings. Turkey droppings are the shape of a small cylinder and are up to about 4 inches long. The Tom and Jake turkeys droppings are typically a few inches long in a straight position with the end curving in a "J" shape. Droppings from hens are typically more spiraled so this is a great way to know what gender of turkey was recently in the area.

As you walk through the woods and fields be sure to take time to not only observe the ground for prints but also look for droppings on the ground. If you find a pile of droppings you should stop to examine them. If the droppings have a wet appearance that means that the droppings are fresh and that the turkey was in the area recently. When the droppings have a dried out appearance that means they are older but it can still be a good sign that turkeys may still be living nearby.

Now let's discuss how to get permission to hunt private land...

Step 9: Getting Permission to Hunt Private Land

Tips for Asking Permission

If you are like me, you do not own hunting land and don't always want to battle other hunters for public land. In addition, many fields prime for turkey hunting often private property. At first it can feel a little uncomfortable to ask other people to use their land for turkey hunting. However, after some experience the process gets much easier. Also, if you get permission to hunt on someone's land one time, they are likely to let you come back again in the future. It can also be advantageous to some property owners to have you hunt their land if they want to thin out the turkey population that might be damaging livestock or being a nuisance on their property.

Tips to get permission to hunt private land:

- Don't be afraid to ask
- Don't wear hunting clothes when approaching them to ask
- Be kind and smile
- Bring a youth hunter if possible
- Tell them exact times you will be there
- Do a favor in return
- Bring them meat or another gift
- Thank them after

Don't Be Afraid to Ask

Something that holds hunters back from finding land to hunt is the fear of asking for permission. People can feel intimidated by asking landowners for permission to hunt on their property but the more you do it the more you get used to it. When you are turned down for permission the primary reason is usually that they already have a friend or family member that hunts the area.

Sample wording to use when asking permission:

- Hello, my name is ___ and I am hoping to do some turkey hunting tomorrow. It seems like you have a great piece of land for turkey hunting. Would it be okay with you if I hunted on your property this weekend?

- Good afternoon, I am looking for a place to turkey hunt with my friend tomorrow. Would it be possible for us to hunt on your land for turkeys for a few hours in the morning?

- Hello, I was driving by your property on my way to town last night and I saw a turkey in your field. I really enjoy turkey hunting and I'm wondering if it would be okay with you if I could hunt here for a few hours this afternoon.

If they say no, don't waste this opportunity to find a hunting spot. Thank them and ask them if they know of any other places nearby that they would suggest trying. They might know another landowner that would allow you to hunt their property or they might know of some good public land for hunting in the area.

Don't Wear Hunting Clothing

I recommend not wearing hunting clothing when you go to ask for permission to hunt on someone's property because it can give the landowners a feeling that you are assuming that you will be able to hunt there. Not all people like or allow hunting so don't assume anything. If you are planning on hunting that same day, at least take off your camouflage clothing. It should not take too much to remove the items that make you look like a hunter. If you are dressed like you are ready to hunt, it can also give them the impression that you may go hunt on their land even if they do not give you permission.

Be Kind and Smile

This should go without saying but if you are polite to the landowner they will more than likely be polite back. Be conscious when you approach the property to put a smile on your face to ensure that you are received as a friendly individual. Do what you can to strike up a conversation with the landowner by asking them some questions such as how long they have lived at the property or what they do for a living. People love to talk about themselves so if you can get the conversation going and let the landowner talk, it will likely improve your chances of getting permission to hunt their land. If they do agree to allow you to hunt on their property, keep the conversation going and ask them where on their property in particular they would recommend hunting. After all, they should know best where the turkeys have been on their property.

Bring a Youth Hunter

Most people have a soft spot for children so if you are planning to hunt with a child it can help to bring them with you when you ask for permission. People who would have said no to you alone may say yes if it means that a child will get the opportunity to experience the outdoors. Another benefit of bringing a child is that it can be a great learning experience for the child. This helps get the child used to speaking to strangers and helps them learn all of the aspects of hunting that will be valuable to them when they start hunting on their own.

Tell Them the Exact Times You Will Be There

To help put the landowners at ease, it is important to let them know exactly when you plan to hunt. If you want to hunt just one morning, tell them that. Or if you want access for an entire weekend, be specific so they are not taken off guard when they see you on their property. This is very important because people will feel more comfortable knowing the exact times that they can expect to see you rather than having you show up at any random time of the day. Never go hunting on someone else's property at a time when you do not have permission.

Do a Favor In Return

Landowners often have work that needs to be done around their property, particularly if they are farmers. Ask them if there are a few projects that you could help out with for an afternoon or two in exchange for hunting on their property. Not only would assisting with these chores be a way to get permission to hunt, it is also a great way to form a relationship with the landowner. The more you get to know them, the more likely they are to let you to continue to hunt there.

Bring Them Meat or Other Small Gifts

Another thing you can ask is if the landowners would like to have some meat in exchange for allowing you to hunt there. Even if they don't hunt, most people may like getting some free meat. This can be a great win-win situation for both parties. Compared to other game animals, turkey is one of the better tasting wild game so there is a good chance they would be interested in sharing some of the meat with you.

Additionally, other small gifts could be a way to say thank you to the landowner for allowing you to use their property. You could bake some cookies in advance or stop at the store on the way and buy some cookies to give them. It does not have to be anything very expensive but something simple can go a long way in letting them know that you appreciate their generosity in allowing you to hunt on their property.

Benefits of Getting Permission Effectively

If you follow these steps and are respectful with those who allow you to hunt their land, you may end up with one or more long-term hunting spots. Be kind when asking, do something in return, and get to know the landowners. The better the connections you make with people, the more likely you will be to build a great network of landowners and have multiple hunting locations that you can use.

The next section covers finding public land for turkey hunting…

Step 10: Finding Public Land to Hunt

Public Land Can Provide Excellent Hunting Opportunities

Similar to private land, with a little effort you can find some great hunting spots available on public land. Again, if you are like me and do not own land to hunt and you have not had any luck getting permission to hunt private land then you may want to look into finding public land to hunt.

Types of public lands available for hunting turkeys:

- Wildlife Management Areas (WMAs)
- State Forests
- Wildlife Refuges
- National Forests
- County Land

Tips about using public land:

- Search online
- Contact your state wildlife office
- Scout out the area in advance
- Be safe

Search Online

With a little online research you will be sure to find some public hunting land within a reasonable driving distance from your home. Simply search online using any of the terms listed above under "Types of public land available for hunting turkeys" followed by your state or county name and there will be sure to be a listing. Each state has different regulations for these areas so if you have questions regarding hunting regulations that are not clearly denoted online, be sure to reach out to your state wildlife office directly.

Contact Your State Wildlife Office

State wildlife officers are usually very friendly people and passionate about the outdoors. Don't be afraid to call the wildlife office and ask them what areas they would suggest nearby for turkey hunting. They want to help people enjoy the outdoors so if you ask, they are going to be happy to assist. Additionally, they understand the importance of properly managing the turkey population in preservation of a healthy environment so they will likely be motivated to help you find a place to hunt turkeys.

Scout the Area in Advance

Once you have a site in mind, if possible, it is great to scout out the area in advance. Try driving to the hunting location a few days prior to hunting and review the territory. Take a walk and note if you see any turkeys. Even if you are unable to physically go to the hunting spot in advance, you can use online resources to help you plan your hunt. Since you may have found this location by looking online for public hunting areas, you can usually find online maps for these public lands. Scan those maps to determine where you will hunt and the route you will take to your hunting spot in advance.

Safety

Safety is the primary thing to be aware of when hunting on public land. Since it is public land, anyone can use this land and there is no way to guarantee that you are alone. It is important to check your surroundings before you shoot. You may find it easy to get caught up in the excitement of shooting and forget what is around you. However, you first want to think about what is in the direction you are shooting can be dangerous at quite a distance can travel a long distance. You need to be one hundred percent sure that there is nobody in the vicinity that could possibly get hit. If you are ever in doubt if you have a safe shot, do not shoot. What makes turkey hunting even more dangerous is the fact that hunters wea camouflage to stay concealed and they are also likely to be using a turkey decoy. This means that someone not paying attention could shoot at a turkey decoy and end up hitting a hidden hunter behind it.

Now let's look at tactics to ensure you start your hunt effectively...

Step 11: Arriving at your Hunting Spot

Your Chances of Success Start as Soon as You Arrive at Your Hunting Spot

It is extremely important to be aware of every little detail when you arrive at your hunting spot and as you walk to the spot where you plan on hunting. Turkeys are wary predators with exceptional eyesight and hearing, this means they will notice things that are out of the ordinary and will do their best to keep a good distance away from humans.

Pay Attention to Little Details to Have Turkey Hunting Success:

- Arrival Path
- Noise
- Timing Your Arrival

Arrival Path

To start off with it a good idea to park a good distance away from your hunting location. Turkeys are able to see and hear vehicles approaching so be sure that you park your vehicle at least several hundred yards away from the location you plan to hunt. Although it is not always fun to walk a long distance, your hunting success can be greatly compromised when parking near your hunting spot.

As you walk from your vehicle to your hunting location you should also pay attention to your cover along the way. What I mean is that you should try and stay as concealed as much as possible as you make your way to the hunting pot. For example, you are often going to be hunting along the tree lines of fields or other open areas. These open areas are great because you can see the turkeys from a good distance away without much obstruction when you want to aim and shoot.

However, these open areas also present the same clear line of sight for turkeys that may be in the area to see you. So you must keep this in mind to improve your hunting success. Most fields are going to have some type tree line or taller grass or vegetation along the edges of the field. By walking along these the natural cover you will keep you a little more concealed rather than blatantly walking across an open field. Of course there is no way to walk to a hunting spot without any chance of being spotted but being aware of movement you are making can help reduce the chances of alerting nearby turkeys.

WALKING TO YOR HUNTING SPOT

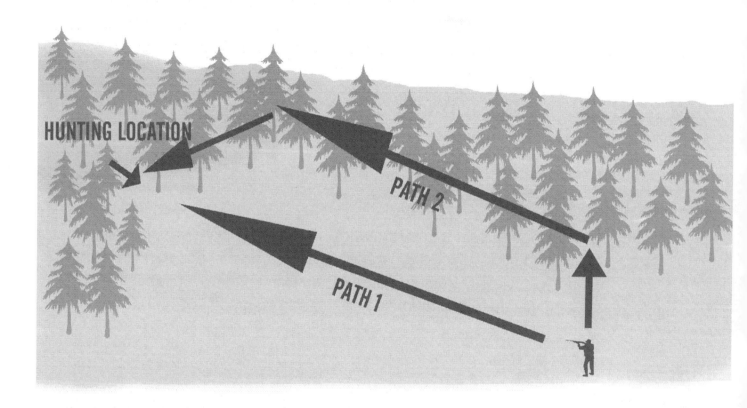

As you can see in the illustration there are two paths that you could use to walk to the hunting location, path 1 or path 2. In the example the hunting location is on the left side of the open field surrounded by trees. The hunter plans on hunting from underneath a few trees there as it should give clear shooting lanes and long viewing distances into the field, it is also where he has recently seen turkeys. Path 1 shows the clearest and easiest path to get to to the hunting spot. This is because anytime you are trying to get somewhere the shortest way is to go in a straight line. Additionally, since this is an open field there is not much in your way so he will likely not be stepping over fallen down trees, battling thick brush or have much difficult terrain to navigate.

However, path 1 has a significant downside in getting to the hunting spot and that is the fact that he will be out in the open for a long period of time while he is walking. This entire time he will be exposed to the sight of any nearby turkeys and will likely scare them away making the long walk entirely wasted. However, what he can do to reduce the chances of being spotted is by using path 2. As you can see with path two there is a tree line that the hunter is going to walk within to stay concealed. He is going to walk several yards into the tree line to use the trees as a natural covering to conceal his movement and body. Path 2 is longer in distance, uphill, and likely has more vegetation to get through making for a more challenging walk but ultimately choosing this path over path 1 can be beneficial.

Of course the illustration is just an example on how you can get to your hunting spot and reduce your chances of being seen. The area you are going to hunt is most likely going to be different but this section is to help you understand the concept that it is best to stay out of wide open spaces as you walk around for turkey hunting. Even though finding paths with more cover are likely to take longer and may be more difficult to navigate, staying out of the sight of turkeys can help keep from scaring the turkeys away.

Noise

Another consideration to keep in mind as you arrive to your hunting spot is controlling the amount of you noise you make. Of course it is pretty much impossible to eliminate all noise but being aware of the noise you are making and doing as much as you can to reduce it will decrease the chances that you scare away turkeys. Turkeys do have a very good hearing so every little bit you do in reducing noise makes a difference.

Be aware of these noise makers:

- Shutting vehicle doors
- Talking

- Stepping on sticks/leaves
- Loading weapons
- Setting up decoys
- Setting up hunting blinds

Timing Your Arrival

The final item to discuss when planning our arrival at your hunting spot is the timing. In general, you should plan to be at your hunting spot well in advance of your legal hunting time. For example, the legal shooting hours in your area might be from ½ hour before sunrise to ½ hour after sunset. In this example I would recommend planning to be sitting and fully setup in your hunting spot at least ½ hour before legal shooting time. This means you will need to plan on leaving much earlier than that to account for the time it will take to walk to your hunting spot and getting any decoys or blinds setup. This is because you will want to allow some time for the area to settle back down before turkeys start getting active. If you are setting up equipment later and the turkeys start moving there is a good chance you will scare them away before ever seeing them. Being setup ½ hour in advance is a good recommended minimum time to be ready but some people prefer to allow an hour or more.

Next we will look at how to use sun to aid in turkey hunting...

Step 12: Sun Impact

Using The Sun to Your Advantage

One tactic you can implement to improve your turkey hunting success is utilizing the sun to help keep yourself concealed from turkeys. As I mentioned earlier, turkeys have incredible sight so anything you can do in order to reduce chances of being seen is a good thing. This means that the sun can play a key factor in turkey hunting success. First off, the sun can be blinding to you as you try and see turkeys. So let's say that you have setup in a way in which the sunrise is going to be coming directly from the direction that you are looking, the East.

This is going to make it difficult for you to see turkeys as you will be blinded by the bright sun in your face.

The second reason is that turkeys are impacted in a similar manner to humans by the bright light of the sun. When turkeys walk directly into the sun it is more challenging for them to see every little detail that is out in front of them due to the bright light. The great thing is that you can use this to your benefit because if you setup with the sun at your back the turkeys will be forced to look into the sun and this can reduce the chances of you being spotted. So as a general rule of thumb setup with the sun to your back and be setup in the shade.

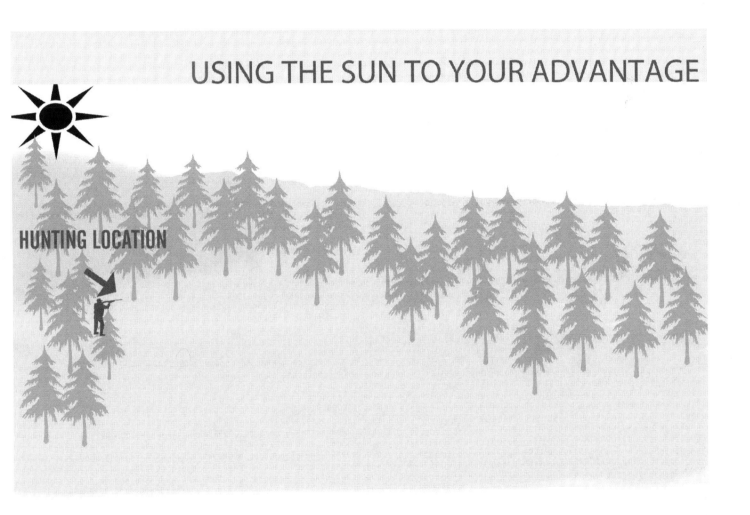

This above example shows how the sun can be of benefit to you as a turkey hunter. You can see that the sun is to the left of the image which means the sun is at the hunters back. As the turkey approaches they will be looking in the direction that the sun is shining from and that can hinder their ability to see anything out in front of them.

In this example I want to show you what to try and avoid in regards to sun. You will now notice is the sun is on the right side of the image. This means that the hunter will be looking directly at the sun as the turkey approaches. Looking in the direction of the sun can be blinding and make it challenging to see the approaching turkey. When it is possible you want to try and setup with the sun at your back.

Now let's take a look at concealment…

Step 13: Concealment

Staying Hidden from Turkeys is Critical for Success

Turkeys, especially older and more experienced Toms, are wary birds and will always be on the lookout for anything that seems out of the ordinary. You must keep this in mind as you determine where you are going to sit and wait for turkeys.

Ways to Stay Hidden:

- Hunting blind
- Natural covering
- Deer/tree stands
- Stay out of direct line of sight
- Avoid body silhouette
- Camouflage & face paint
- Ghillie suit
- Smell

Hunting Blind

A simple yet effective way to stay concealed from the sight of turkeys is by using a ground blind. Ground blinds are easily transportable which make them a great option if you want to try hunting several different places. Some people like to move locations if they have been calling for an hour or so without any response from turkeys. These blinds are like little tents with a zip open door and windows for shooting. When hunting from a ground blind you will want to bring some type of chair with to sit on because sitting on the ground for any length of time will not be comfortable.

One of the biggest benefits of ground blinds is that you can place them in high traffic turkey areas that do not have much for other natural covering around. For example, if there is an open field without much for trees or shrubs the blind can be a good option. Simply try and find a spot that is relatively close to some trails that you have found frequented by turkeys that lead out into the field.

There are a few other benefits to ground blinds which include the fact that it will keep you out of the elements and comfortable. Like I mentioned these are like little tents so when it is windy, raining, snowing or cold outside these blinds will help you stay somewhat protected from the elements and much more comfortable during your hunt. The last benefit to mention about ground blinds is their low cost. You can find them on sale at hunting stores for around $40. Of course you can buy more expensive ones but for something to get you started an entry level blind should do the trick.

Natural Concealment

Utilizing your surroundings to keep you out of the sight of turkeys can be another great way for concealment. Often times you will be hunting turkeys that are in an open field or prairie with a decoy or multiple decoys and then you will be sitting on the side of the field to stay concealed. The good thing about hunting fields is that these fields will often be lined with trees, tall grass, fence lines or even woods that you can use to keep hidden.

For example, the field might have a fence line on the side of the field and then some woods on the other side of the fence. This can be a great situation as you could sit below the trees with fence in front of you as you look out over the field. The fence in front of you should provide some additional cover but you should still have good shooting lanes as turkeys walk in the fields.

With natural concealment you can get very creative on what to use to keep yourself covered. Take for example when hunting a prairie that is very hilly, what you could do is lie down on the top of one of the hills with a lot of camouflage on and then look out over the rest of the field from this higher elevation. The natural curvature of the hill can help keep you hidden as long as you stay towards the back portion of the crest of the hill so the hill keeps you mostly concealed.

Deer/Tree Stands

The areas that turkeys live in are often areas that deer live in as well. In pretty much any place that has deer there are likely to be some people that hunt deer. A great benefit of this is that deer hunters often use elevated deer stands for hunting and those deer stands can work well for hunting turkeys. There are a variety of deer stands such as ladder stands which is pictured above but people also use tripod stands which are stands that sit on a large tripod style base so they do not need to be placed in a tree.

Regardless of the style of deer stands that are available to you on the land you hunt these could all be useful for hunting turkeys. One clear benefit of using a deer stand is elevation that it provides you. Many deer stands are 8-15 feet up in the air and by sitting in them it will greatly increase the distance that you will be able to see turkeys. Another benefit of being high up in the air is that it takes you out of the direct line of sight of turkeys. This is because turkeys will be looking at ground level as they approach your decoys. However, due to the elevation you will need to be aware that you remain within effective shooting range to the turkeys.

Of course if you do use a tree stand you still need to be aware of concealment so you still should have camouflage covering every part of your body. Also, and depending on the stand you have it might not provide much to hide your movement. So when you do hunt out of a tree stand it is still important to not move very much because even though you are elevated in the air it is still possible that the turkeys could see you particularly if you are moving around a lot.

Avoid Body Silhouette

Another tip to stay concealed from the sight of turkeys is to avoid a body silhouette. This goes along with having your back to the sun which I described earlier but what I am talking about is if you are standing or sitting in a location where there is nothing behind you then there is a much higher chance that a turkey can see you compared to when you have something behind you to cover the outline of your body. Take the above picture for an example. It is pretty easy to see the person standing on the left side of the image because the sun is shining and it creates an outline of the person that can be seen from a long distance away.

In contrast, if the person was sitting directly in front of the large rock it would be much more difficult to see them as they would have something behind them to help cover their silhouette. So the quick and simple tip about this is to always make sure that there is something behind you so you do not stick out like a sore thumb. You could sit in front of rocks, trees, bushes, fences or pretty much anything else that is at least as big as you are so there is something blocking out your body outline.

Ghillie Suit

For hunters who really want to get concealed well even when there is not much surrounding cover you could consider investing in a ghillie suit. A guillie suit takes camouflage to another level because the suit has fake grass covering the entire suit allowing you to blend into vegetation extremely well. For example, you could lay on the ground in the open with a ghillie suit and wait for a turkey to get extremely close before you pop up and shoot. Of course laying on the ground for an extended period of time is not going to be very comfortable but if you are up for some close action and are not worried about being uncomfortable for a while this could be a great option for you.

Smell

Now that I have probably made you a little nervous regarding the great eyesight and hearing that that turkeys have there is good news that there is one trait that turkeys do not have which is a sense of smell. Turkeys are really not able to smell you even if you have to put on bug spray so away you do not have to worry about scaring them off from the scent. This is a stark contrast to may other game that you might hunt such as deer where you have to go to great lengths to remove any human odor or you will have no chance of getting deer to come close enough.

Now let's discuss using decoys to fool turkeys...

Step 14: Decoying

Use Decoys to Attract Turkeys

Decoys are a great tool for attracting turkeys. In most cases you will be calling for turkeys which I will discuss further in "Step 16 Calling" but it is important to note that using a decoy of some sort along with calling is very important in bagging turkeys. This is because as a turkey approaches the location where they hear the calling sounds coming they are looking to validate by seeing the turkey that is making the sound.

Make sure that you place the decoys in a location that is highly visible to the approaching turkeys. You should try and place them on higher spots in the field such as ridges, mounds or clearings in the field where the decoy can be easily seen from any direction. This is critical as you want the turkey to see the decoy as they come to the sound of the calls. Now let's take a look at a handful of options that you can use for turkey decoys.

Examples of turkey decoys:

- Tom decoys
- Jake decoys
- Hen decoys
- Fan decoy
- Place decoys out of direct line of sight
- Hunting without a decoy

Tom Decoys

One option that you have to get tom turkeys to come to your hunting location is to use a tom decoy. Essentially with a tom decoy you are using the territorial behavior that turkeys have in order to elicit Toms in the area to come and chase off the intruder. Sometimes it might be just one tom coming to chase off the intruder and sometimes there might be two or more. In addition, to make this scene even more lifelike you could place a hen decoy next to this decoy or directly in front of the decoy in a lying position as if it is ready to breed. Although it can be effective to utilize tom decoys there are times when it can backfire. The reason why sometimes it could not work is if the turkeys in the area are scared off from the decoy. For example, if there are jakes or even smaller toms nearby and they see a much larger and more dominant turkey it is possible that they will just leave the area because they feel they would not be able to win a fight with the larger bird.

Jake Decoys

Another option for decoys is a jake decoy which can be used in a similar method to the tom decoys. Here you can use hen decoys in addition to the jake decoy in order to show that the pair are potentially going to mate. Even though this setup can be similar to how you would setup a tom decoy with a hen, the big difference is that when tom turkeys see jakes they are likely to be larger and be willing to be more aggressive to a jake and scare it off. You may find this particularly effective to pull in some of the smaller less dominant toms that had been chased away from hens by larger toms. These smaller toms may work into a jake decoy setup due to their size difference as they are still larger than a jake and feel that they could fight it off.

Hen Decoys

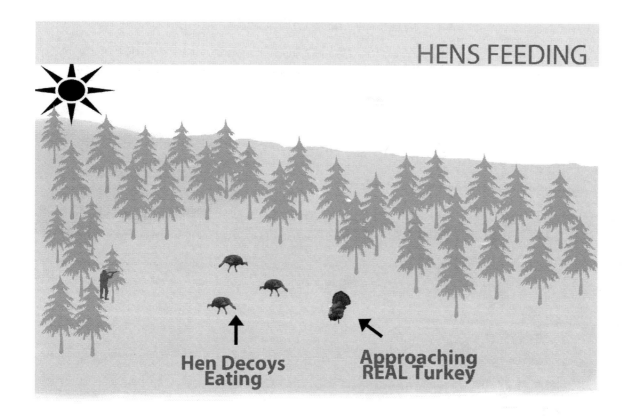

Hen decoys are very popular to use for turkey hunting, particular during mating season. Basically, a hen decoy is used to lure in nearby Toms and Jakes who are looking for a mate. Actually, it is not uncommon for more than one male turkey to approach the female turkey decoy at a time. When placing the hen decoys you have several options for setting them up. First you could setup the hens as if there are a group of hens out in a field eating. This is a common scene in the mid morning and afternoon. Toms may see these hens comfortably feeding and find this as a good opportunity to come and attempt to breed with one of them. This example is outlined in the illustration above.

Another option is to have one or two hen decoys placed on the ground in a breeding position. Or if you have a pair of hen decoys one could be placed on the ground and the other could be in an upright position. Regardless if you have one or two on the ground the intent is to indicate that a hen is ready to breed and can be a very enticing image for toms and jakes in the area to approach.

The final option with the hens is to mix them with tom or jake decoys as I previously mentioned when discussing tom and jake decoys. When you do this you place the hen next to or in front of the male decoy in order to show that breeding might be happening soon. Then if when a tom or jake see this they may come to the scene to fight off the other male turkey and claim the hen for himself to breed with.

Fan Decoys

Fan decoys have increased in popularity as of the recent years because of the excitement they provide when you use them. Essentially a fan turkey decoy is a two dimensional cut outline of a turkey with an image of a turkey printed on one side. On the back side of the decoy there is a handle for the hunter to use to hold the decoy. With this decoy the hunter crouches behind the decoy and then works his way to nearby turkeys. Basically the user of the decoy is imitating the look of a turkey approaching other turkeys and stays hidden behind the decoy while he works his way closer to the real turkeys. Once the hunter is close enough to the real turkeys he pops up from behind the decoy and takes a shot at the unsuspecting birds.

Decoy Facing

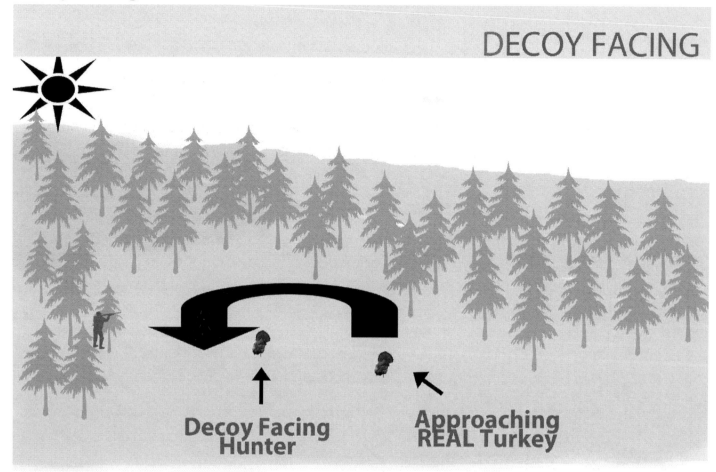

Another tip to try when you use tom and jake decoys is to face the decoy towards the hunter. The reason you would want to try this is that the real tom turkey typically wants to look the turkey he is going to fight with directly in the face when he is getting ready to fight. By putting the tom/jake decoy facing you it forces the approaching turkey to circle the decoy and come around in front of it to look at the decoy in the face. When he does this it will make the distance between you and the real turkey shorter. Also, when he turns to face the decoy he will have his back to you which will reduce the chances of you being spotted. Of course this may not happen every time but it can be effective for those toms looking for a fight.

Hunting Without Decoys

Although decoys can be very effective in bringing turkeys into range it is important to note that it is not always necessary to use a decoy so if you do not have one or it is not in your budget yet to buy one you should not let that hinder you from turkey hunting. Turkey decoys have not always been legal in all areas and people had plenty of success hunting turkeys without them. Without decoys your calling techniques will typically need to be fairly good as you cannot rely on the turkey coming to the decoy so you will need to entice the birds to come to you through communication alone. One thing you may want to try without decoys is being setup in a location that is not visible from a long distance.

For example, when you are hunting with decoys being in a place where the turkeys can see the decoy from a long distance is a great idea as the turkey will be able to visually see where the sounds are coming from. However, without a decoy being in a spot that is a little less visible can be effective as any turkeys in the area will need to come much closer to check out what is going on so the birds will be a lot closer before they do not see another turkey present in the area.

Now let's take a look at calling for turkeys…

Step 15: Call Types and Sounds

Turkey Calls to Grab Attention

Communicating with turkeys by calling them in can be a satisfying and unique experience. With some practice you can become effective at drawing turkeys close which will greatly improve your success. In this this section I'll give you an overview of each type of call and how it could be beneficial to you. I will also provide you information on some of the basic call sounds that are used and provide you resources for learning how to call.

Types of Turkey Calls

- Box Calls
- Shaker Calls
- Mouth Calls
- Slate Calls
- How to Learn Turkey Calling
- Electronic Calls

Box Calls

A box call is a call that looks like a small wooden box that you hold in your hand with a handle. The handle is called a "paddle" and is attached to the top of the wooden box and held in place by a mechanism that allows the user to move the paddle back and forth across the top of the box. As the paddle is moved across the top it rubs against the box and creates the sounds of turkeys. For a beginner the box call is probably going to be one of your best choices as they are relatively easy to operate yet they still make a variety realistic sounding turkey calls.

Shaker Calls

Another relatively easy to use call for turkey hunting is a shaker call. Shaker calls are typically made out of a rubber material. To operate the call you simply grab the bottom side of the call with your hand and shake the call back and forth vigorously. As you shake the call it makes gobble sounds of turkeys. Not only are these calls fairly easy to use but they are usually inexpensive costing about $20 for most varieties. Some of these calls also allow you to tap on the top of the call to get a turkey "cut" sound or a variety of other sounds depending on the specific call you purchase.

Slate Calls

A slate call is a call that consists of two pieces. One piece is the slate surface itself which is a round flat circle, similar in size and appearance to a coaster for a cup. On the top and bottom of the circle there is a layer of slate, aluminum, copper, Teflon and a variety of other materials that that make the surface in which you rub against to make the sounds. The second piece of the call is called a striker which sort of looks like a pencil that you rub across the surface of the slate to make sounds through the vibration. Based on the way you rub the striker across the surface it will make a wide range of turkey sounds. Although these calls are probably going to take a little bit of time to master, with just a little bit of practice you should be able to make calls that are realistic enough to pull in turkeys.

Mouth Calls

Mouth calls are one of the staples to turkey hunting and have been around for many years in the turkey hunting world. Basically, they are a plastic molded piece that you put on the roof of your mouth and use your tongue and different blowing techniques to make various turkey calls. They almost resemble the top portion of a retainer that someone would get from an orthodontist use to straighten their teeth. Depending on how you blow the mouth calls they can make a wide range of sounds like the cluck, yelp and purr sounds to name a few.

One consideration with mouth calls is that they can take a little time to get used to. However, once you get the calling down they can be very realistic in sound and you may find it personally satisfying to call turkeys in with a mouth call versus other call types. Mouth calls are usually one of the least expensive call types with many of them being in the range of $10. The other benefit of using a mouth call is that it frees up your hands for shooting. You can simply keep the call in our mouth as you work a turkey into range and when you are ready you will be able to shoot without having to put a call down to pick up your gun.

How to Learn to Call for Turkeys

Because there are so many different call types to choose from and each call operates differently it is important to have some resources on how to learn to call. In fact, entire books have been written on turkey calling and operating different call types. To learn more about how to use the call I would recommend some looking at some of the following resources.

Resources to learn how to call for turkeys:
- Owner's manual may come with the call for some basic tips
- CDs sold at hunting stores
- YouTube videos (simply search for turkey calling videos)
- Online hunting forums
- Fellow hunters

Electronic Calls

One final call type I want to mention is an electronic call. Basically an electronic call is a speaker system that you can place out in the field that plays real recorded turkey sounds. Many models allow you to use a remote control to turn the unit on and off so you do not have to go out into the field to operate the speaker. Electronic turkey calls range in cost from about $40 to $400 or more but can be worth the investment. However, you must note that many states ban the use of electronic callers for turkeys. So before you purchase or use an electronic caller be sure that you check your states regulations regarding their use.

The nice thing about electronic calls is that most models have a huge amount of sounds they can reproduce. This means that if you test one turkey sound and with a push of a button and you can get a completely different turkey sound to try and entice a nearby turkey. Another advantage of electronic calls is that there is not nearly the learning curve that there is with other call types. With an electronic call all you need to do is simply push the button on the remote and you can turn on the call with extremely lifelike sound. This ease of use makes electronic calls a great option for beginning turkey hunters.

However, please note that even if they are legal to use in your area many people frown upon the use of electronic calls because they feel that the time should be taken to learn how to call turkeys without the assistance of electronics. In addition, you may notice more personal satisfaction being able to call turkeys with a manually controlled call compared to an electronic call. You are welcome to make your own decision to use an electronic call, if legal in your area, but for those who are open to using them they can be an effective way to bag turkeys as you work your way to learning to use other call types.

Call Sounds and Timing

When calling for turkeys it is important to know that there is wide range of sounds that can bring turkeys to your hunting location. Additionally, each type of call sound has its own purpose to create a specific response from the nearby turkeys. For example, a soft hen purr can let nearby toms know that the hen is calm and open to having a tom approach her. The purrs are also often made when the hens are feeding safely.

Types of turkey calls:

- **Gobble-** One of the most commonly recognizable sounds made by a turkey. It is a simple gobble sound made by a tom to let hens know that he is in the area.
- **Yelp-** This is known as one of the locator type calls meaning it can be a great call to make to see if other turkeys are in the area. Turkeys often make this sound as they feed throughout the day or they will also make it in a more rapid succession if they are lost and trying to find other turkeys.
- **Purr-** Using this type of call can be effective in getting the toms to make a final approach to your hen decoy. Soft purrs indicate that the hen is relaxed while eating and is a great way for the hen to let the tom know it is ok to approach her.
- **Cut-** Another effective call to bring in toms. The sound replicates a hen that is very excited and calling the tom to come to her.

- **Fly Down Cackle-** This is a sound to let tom turkeys know that a hen has flown down off the roost and is in the area.

I do want to point out that this is a list of some of your most common turkey call sounds along with the basic purpose that each one serves in successful turkey hunting. Please be aware that there is wide range of variations to each of these as well as many other calls that can be effective as you expand your turkey hunting calling skills. As a beginning to intermediate turkey hunter I would recommend that you start with the basic call types as you work to get experience and success.

After you start mastering some of these calls then it is great to add some additional sounds to your turkey calling vocabulary. However, it is best to not complicate things as you get into the sport and risk becoming frustrated. There is a ton to learn with turkey hunting so start to build your skills and expand from there. Think of it like riding a bike, when you first learn it is about the basics of balancing, starting and stopping. You do not start off riding wheelies and jumping curbs. Those are all fun things to add down the road but you must first start with a good foundation before expanding into more advanced tactics.

Calling Frequency

Another consideration with calling turkeys is the calling frequency as you work turkeys into your hunting area. What I mean by calling frequency is how often you call for turkeys. You could elect to continually call for turkeys until you get one to come in or you may only call a few times in hopes of pulling in turkeys. What is the perfect amount of calling? Well this is really where experience and trial and error comes into play. Some people call for turkeys every few minutes while other turkey hunters call just a handful of times per hour.

People have had plenty of success with both methods and it is really up to you to try out and see what works best for you and your area or even the specific turkey you have near you for that hunt. For example, if you have a very vocal turkey responding to you with every call you make then it might be good to keep calling back every few minutes. However, you may have times where the calls are more intermittent and it can work to cycle your calling and give 10 - 15 minutes in between calls. Again, there is really no perfect answer to the amount of calling because people have had success with all frequencies and each individual turkey may react differently.

What If You Don't Get Any Response?
There will be some times when you call for turkeys and do not get a response. Hopefully you have used the tips about scouting your hunting area in advance to do your best to confirm that there are turkeys around. However, there will be times when the turkeys have moved out or are just not cooperating that day. It is important to give each hunting spot a good amount of time calling to see if you get a response. There will be times that it takes longer for turkeys to react or come within range to be able to hear your calls but about 30 minutes to an hour or so can be an appropriate amount of time. Some people may choose to sit a little longer before they call it quits for that spot.

If possible try and have 2-3 hunting spots scouted out and ready to hunt. It is going to take more time and effort to have a few spots lined up but this will give you some great flexibility on the times you do get out hunting. If you setup at one of your hunting locations and call for a while without response you can then pack up and head to the next location.

It is also important to note that you will not always get a response from a turkey immediately but it does not mean that one is not coming to you. It is ideal when you get a response from a Tom by them gobbling back to you right away when you call. However, sometimes the tom will not make respond at all but he is still headed your way. Then when you are least expecting it he appears out of nowhere or he finally gobbles back when he is very close. This is why it is important to give each location some time to see if a turkey is coming your way. You may not always hear them coming but it does not mean a turkey is not right around the corner. This is also why you keep as still as possible during all times of turkey hunting because even if you do not see a turkey it is possible that one has snuck up on you and if you move you are likely to scare it off.

Now let's talk about still hunting…

Step 16: Still Hunting

Bring the Turkeys to You

One of the most common ways to hunt turkeys is the still method which is when a hunter sets up for hunting in one spot and calls to bring the turkeys within shooting distance. This can be an enjoyable and relaxing way to hunt turkeys because once you get your hunting spot, decoys setup and are in position you simply get to sit back to call turkeys and enjoy the outdoors as you wait for turkeys to come.

Considerations for Still Hunting:

- Shooting distance
- Find a funnel
- Create your own trails
- Scanning for turkeys

Shooting distance

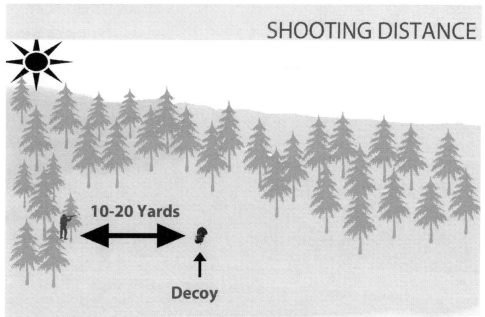

When you are trying to figure out your exact spot you will sit for your still turkey hunting you want to be aware of the shooting distance. As I had mentioned earlier, the effective shooting distance for many shotguns is around 40 yards. Of course there are some situations where the shot could reach further than that but the general recommendation is to ensure that your shots are 40 yards or less and preferably around the 20 yard range to ensure maximum effectiveness.

So as you plan out the spot you will be sitting in be sure you think about where the turkeys are likely to come from. If you have scouted the area in advance you might have actually seen where the turkeys frequently walk so be sure that you get within a short distance to that spot. Even if you have not seen the turkeys during scouting you should be able to identify where common trails are that lead out of the woods or walking paths in the field that you have identified by seeing turkey footprints.

Take the image as an example of this suggestion of trying to stay within 10-20 yards of the decoy. You can see that the decoy is placed 20 yards away from the hunter so that means that if any turkey approaches the decoy and is in between the hunter and the decoy it will be well within shotgun range. Even if a turkey approaches and is on the far side of the decoy the hunter should still be able to make an effective shot as it will still be a shot of less than 40 yards. If you will be hunting with a bow you will want to narrow down these ranges a little bit more to ensure that you can hit the turkey with your arrow.

Find a funnel

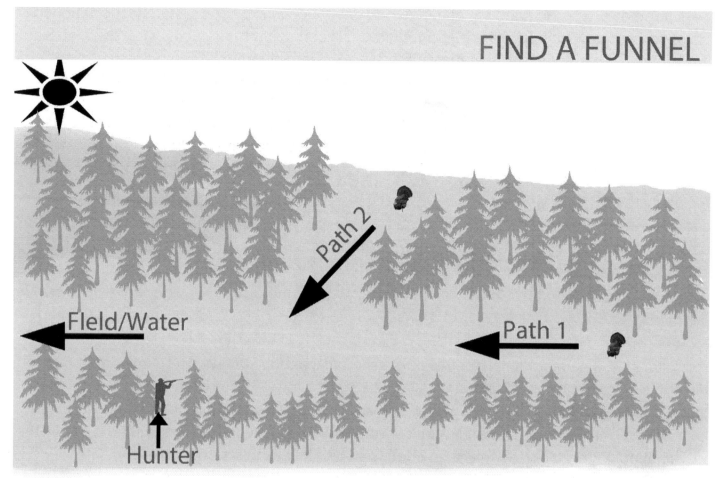

This can go hand in hand with shooting distance but it can also be effective to find a funnel to hunt near. This technique is more for use when you are hunting inside of a woods rather on open field. Essentially what you want to do is observe any natural trails in the woods that are frequented by turkeys and find spots where 2-3 trails funnel down to 1 trail. This could be a place where trails combine as they begin to make its way out into an open area or to water.

Those trails will act as natural funnels because the turkeys will be coming from various directions but ultimately to get to the field or open water there is only one clear path to walk through. Positioning yourself by paths like these can improve your chances of success because any turkeys walking that direction will only have one choice for a path to walk through so you can ambush them as they come down the path.

Create Your Own Trails

Depending on the area you are hunting and the trail system nearby it can sometimes be effective to make your own trails. For example, there may be trails running nearby throughout the woods but in this case none of them lead out into the field nearby where you plan to hunt. What you could do in this situation is clear a path or two from the trails in the woods and have those paths lead out into the field near where you are hunting. You would want to do this a few weeks in advance of when you plan to hunt due to the amount of noise you will make and to allow the turkeys to get used to this new trail system. In order to accomplish the task you could use a yard trimmer such as a weed wacker or even a chainsaw depending on how thick of brush you need to cut down in order to clear a path.

Scanning for Turkeys

When hunting for turkeys you will want to be continually scanning the area for turkeys. A good strategy to implement is to scan from the left to the right and keep doing this at varying distances. For example, start by looking to the far left side of your hunting spot about 20 yards out and then scan to the right all around the same distance. Once you scan until you are looking all of the way to your right increase the distance you are looking, say to 40 yards, yards and then back to the left. Keep slowly increasing the distance you scan by 10-20 yards with each turn of your head. Once you reach the limit of your hunting area then start the process back over. By focusing in on specific distances it can help you look closer for turkeys in that area rather then trying to look at an area all at once.

Now let's identify tips for hunting turkeys with a buddy…

Step 17: The Buddy System

Use a Buddy to Improve Success

Hunting for turkeys can be a great way to enjoy the outdoors by yourself but it can also be a fun way to spend some time with friends or family. Not only is it fun to share the experience but hunting with a partner can also help improve your success rate.

Benefits of hunting with a partner:

- Calling
- Two guns
- Extra set of eyes
- Be safe

Calling

One huge benefit to hunting with a buddy is calling for the turkeys. When you are hunting by yourself it will be up to you to do all of the calling for the turkeys so if you are using a slate call, box call or shaker call your hands will be tied up using the call rather than holding your weapon in preparation for the turkey to get within shooting range. When you bring a buddy with you can share this responsibility and tag team turkeys.

For example, your buddy could start off doing all the calling and this will allow you to focus completely on any approaching turkeys. After you have bagged a turkey you can switch responsibilities and give your buddy the chance to shoot the next turkey. Sometimes a pair of turkeys will come in together and the first person can shoot the first turkey and the 2nd turkey will stay around for a little bit allowing the person who was doing the calling an opportunity to shoot as well. Even if it does not work out where both hunters shoot a turkey on one day, you could swap days until each hunter has had the chance to harvest a turkey.

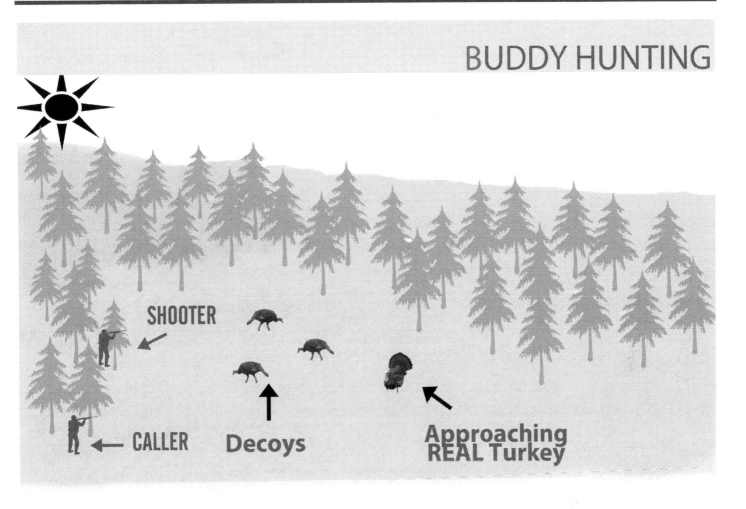

Another benefit when hunting with a buddy is that you can hunt from different locations and have one of the hunters call for the turkey while the other hunter is the shooter. This allows the sounds to be coming from a slightly different location then where the hunter is positioned. This way if the approaching turkey is eyeing up the location of the sounds the hunter with the weapon will not be directly where the turkey is. This can allow the shooter to get the weapon raised and ready to fire with less chances of being spotted.

Two Guns

Another benefit of having your buddy with for your turkey hunting trip is that you will now have two guns rather than one. Particularly if you are using mouth calls you could both have guns ready to shoot. This could be useful if two turkeys approach at one time. The hunters could each pick a turkey and at the same time shoot so you hopefully bag both of the birds.

Additionally, with two guns one hunter misses their shot at the turkey the other hunter could be prepared to follow up with a quick second shot at the turkey before it runs out of shooting range

Extra Set of Eyes

Turkeys can sometimes be challenging to spot, especially in areas covered with a lot of natural vegetation such as trees, brush and tall grass. They can also challenging to pick out when you are trying to spot them from long distances. This makes it beneficial to have a buddy with as you can both be on the lookout for approaching turkeys as one of you may see a turkey that the other hunting partner missed.

Try sitting next to each other or even back to back. This way you can each focus on covering a certain area while the other hunter looks at a completely different area. You can essentially double the area that you can scout by adding a buddy. However, it can also be useful to trade off areas that you are looking at. What I mean is that after 10 or 15 minutes if you do not see turkeys you could alternate the spots you are watching. This can be effective because after looking at one area for a long time you may miss something where switching things up and having a fresh pair of eyes look over the area could help spot the cunning turkeys.

Be Safe

Anytime you are using weapons it is very important to keep safety in mind. You never want to have a fun hunting situation turn into an unfortunate event and have someone get hurt. This aspect is increased when you are hunting with a buddy compared to hunting by yourself because you want to make sure that you never fire your weapon in the direction that your buddy is located.

It is important to always tell each other where you are going to be hunting from and plan out your hunting locations in advance and communicate this well with each other. Even when you have discussed hunting spots with your buddy you should still be cautious when you are preparing to take a shot. Something may have happened that caused your partner to move from their planned hunting spot so be sure that you scan around the area that you are shooting at to ensure nobody is in that vicinity. If you are ever unsure if you are taking a safe shot, do not shoot. It is better to miss out on a shot at a turkey over injuring a friend.

Now let's identify effective turkey stalking techniques…

Step 18: Stalking Turkeys

Actively Walking to Find Turkeys can Produce Great Results

Stalking turkeys means that you walk through the woods and fields to actively find turkeys. Although this will require more work to hunt turkeys compared to the still method, with some practice and this can be effective way to bag some extra turkeys.

Critical Components to Turkey Stalking:

- Plan your route
- Walk quietly
- Stop often and observe
- Always be ready to shoot

Plan Your Route

As you get ready to actively hunt for turkeys it is important to plan your route. You should think about the area you are going to be hunting and try and strategize what the best way will be to cover all of the area in the most effective manner. If it is a small woods you could walk down ½ of the woods and when you get to one end you turn around and walk back down the other ½ of the woods. For those times when you are hunting larger woods you could try to zig-zag through the woods and eventually get from one side of the woods to the other. Just critically think about the best way will be to cover as much area as possible. You should also think about the high traffic areas for turkeys. Areas near young vegetation, berries, nuts and other food sources are places that you should be sure to check. Additionally, areas near water can be effective as the turkey will eventually need to drink.

Walk Quietly

As you actively hunt for turkeys it is best to try and walk as quietly as possible. You will want to lift your feet up completely off the ground with each step and take small calculated steps. As you set your foot down, let your heel make contact with the ground first and then gently allow the rest of your foot down. It is inevitable that you will make some noise as there will be branches and dry leaves that you cannot avoid stepping on but by consciously walking quietly you will greatly reduce the amount of noise you make.

Walking quietly helps you get closer to the turkeys before they take off. If you go crashing through the woods without any regard to how much noise you make it is likely that you will kick up turkeys that are too far away to shoot at or you will never see them at all as they will leave before you have a chance to see them. Being mindful of your noise should allow you to get to a reasonable shooting range before the birds are scared up, remember that hearing and sight are the turkeys best defense mechanisms so you must take every effort to approach quietly.

Stop Often and Observe

To ensure you have the best chances of seeing and hearing turkeys you will want to stop every 5-10 steps and actively look around. When you are walking it is hard to hear turkeys because of the amount of noise you make while walking but when you stop it should get much quieter. Listen closely for anything that may sound like a turkey such as leaves crunching or branches breaking. You may even hear them gobble or yelp.

In addition to listening, you should also scan your surroundings carefully. Be particularly aware of any movement that you see and watch that area closely to see if it was a turkey. Start by looking one direction, such as your far left, and then scan carefully from left to right. After you are looking all of the way to your right scan back to your left again. It is beneficial to do this a few times each time you stop to be sure you spot any turkeys in the area. If you think you saw something move, ensure you give it a few moments before you move because if it was a turkey they will likely resume moving shortly and you should be able to spot them.

Mix In Some Calling

In addition to stopping every 5-10 steps to observe if there are any turkeys in the area it can also work well to try calling for turkeys frequently. You might not call every 5-10 steps but after walking for 5-10 minutes you can try finding a spot to sit down and call for a few minutes. Pull out your call and try a few different call types. If you get a response within a few minutes then hold tight and see if you can get the turkey to come close. If you do not get a response after a few minutes then you can get up and continue walking.

Always be Ready to Shoot

When walking through the woods as well as open fields you should hold your gun in a manner that allows you to quickly get into shooting position. Hold the stock near the trigger in one hand and the other hand near the base of the barrel where you normally hold your gun when shooting. I can't stress enough how critical it is to the success of turkey hunting to be able to shoot quickly if you happen to scare one up from a spot you were not suspecting one to be at.

After turkey hunting for even a day you will notice how fast they are and how fast they can run out of range. Even when you find a turkey in a close distance the shots are still challenging because of all of the trees, branches and leaves that can be in the way. The quicker you can shoot, the higher your chances of hitting your turkey.

Of course you will want to pay attention to safety when you are walking with a loaded gun. Always be sure to keep the barrel pointed away from any other hunters and yourself. When you are traveling over logs and other difficult terrain you need to further increase your safety awareness in case you trip.

Now let's look at some effective shooting strategies when turkey hunting...

Step 19: Deadly Shot Placement

Successfully Bag Your Turkey

When you finally have a turkey come into sight it is one of those moments that makes your heart race. This moment can be brief so you need to be ready to quickly take action to bag the turkey. You must always be prepared because turkeys are leery birds and as soon as they notice anything out of order they will quickly run away and be out of effective shooting distance. Use these tips to make the most out of your shooting opportunities.

Shooting tips:

- Practice shooting before the hunting season
- Know your pattern
- Be patient
- Select a clear shooting lane
- Shot placement
- Improving shot accuracy
- Learn from missed shots

Practice Shooting Before the Hunting Season

If you have never been turkey hunting or if you are having difficulty hitting turkeys then it might be a good idea to get in some target practice before you head out to the field. If you do not have your own land one of the easiest and most cost effective ways to practice shooting is to visit a firing range. Chances are you live within a half hour of a firing range where you can pay a fee to practice shooting. This is usually inexpensive as you can buy a time slot, usually in hour or half hour increments, for less than $20. This minimal investment could greatly improve your success on your next hunting trip.

However, it is not always necessary to go to a firing range. If you own your own land you could certainly use that to practice. Or if the land that you are going to be doing your turkey hunting on is available for target practice you could use that as well. The one thing to keep in mind is if you do plan on target practicing on the same land that you will be hunting on I would recommend doing it many days or even weeks in advance. This is because it is likely the shooting may scare away turkeys so do this in advance to leave enough time for the turkeys to settle down and return to the area.

Know Your Pattern

An important piece of shooting turkeys is knowing your shotgun pattern. Essentially a shotgun pattern is how tight r loose your BBs are dispersed when hitting a target. Shotguns will pattern differently based on the distance to the target, choke tube used and shotgun shell used. All of these factors will impact how the BBs hit a target or turkey at a specific distance. As you go out target practicing before the hunting season it is important to take test shots at a variety of different distances.

You can go to a local sporting goods store and buy a turkey target kit for $10 or less. The kit will have several printed pieces of paper with turkey heads on them. What you do is set these targets out at varying ranges, usually in 10 yard increments to see how well the BBs hit the target. It is important to ensure that the distances you plan on shooting turkeys at have plenty of BBs on the target at that specific distance. For example if 35 yards is where you notice that there are not many BBs still hitting the target than you should plan for shots that will be less than 35 yards. Some of the target practice kits are designed where you can write the distance on each target to record how many BBs hit the target. This way you can compare the shots taken at each distance and see what distances will be lethal with your exact gun and shell selection.

Be Patient

I also encourage you to be patient when you are hunting for turkeys, particularly with shot selection. The temptation to shoot right away when you see a turkey can be strong but you should hold back until you have a clear shot at the turkey and that the shot is within the effective range of your weapon. Sometimes you may notice the turkeys head directly to the decoy and get quickly within shooting range. However, other times the turkeys will walk around for a while as they investigate what is going on. They are simply checking out the sounds and the turkeys that they see before heading directly at towards the decoy. Again, as tempting as it might be to shoot right away, it is critical to be patient and hold tight until you have a high percentage shot. If you shoot to early you will end up wasting a lot of ammunition and scaring off many turkeys that you would have eventually had a better shot at.

The other part of being patient is knowing when to raise your gun or draw your bow. If you are able to see the turkey coming from a long way away it might be possible to get the gun ready right away. However, if you are hunting with a bow it is pretty much impossible to hold the bow in a drawn position for a long period of time while you wait for the turkeys to get closer. What you will want to do, if possible, is wait for the turkey to turn its back to you or at least to turn to the side before you draw your bow or raise your gun. This way the chances of the turkey seeing you move will be greatly reduced.

Select a Clear Shooting Lane

Waiting for a clear shooting lane goes hand in hand with being patient. This is particularly the case for hunting in the woods compared to a field where there wont be much obstruction. You want to try to get into a position where you can see the turkey and not have a lot of grass, trees, branches, rocks or anything blocking the way of your shot. This is easy to say but in reality it is difficult, especially if you are hunting in a woods covered with tall vegetation. This is where some skill and practice come into play.

Many times you can only see part of the turkey. The turkey may just have its head sticking around the back side of a rock or the turkey might have half of its body covered by tall grass. Now is when you need to decide whether or not to take the shot. If you have a shot at the turkey, regardless of how small of a portion of the turkey it might be, you need to decide if this is going to be your best opportunity to shoot this turkey.

If you think that this is your best chance then go ahead and take the shot. However, if you feel that you may get a better shot if you wait then go ahead and wait. Shooting and missing is likely going to cause the turkey to run away and you may not get any other chances to shoot that turkey. Also, a shot may scare off any other turkeys in the area as well so it is just important to make your best educated guess if you should wait. If you do miss try and not get to down on yourself as missed shots do happen. There is no guarantee you would have had a better shot opportunity had you waited so just trust you made the best judgment you could at the time.

Shot Placement

Now that a turkey is in shooting range let's discuss where you should attempt to place your shot. The two primary shot locations you want to focus on when shooting turkeys are the head and the neck areas. Both of these have some advantages and downsides so let's examine each option.

Head

An accurately placed shot at the head of a turkey will provide a very quick and lethal kill. This is because the turkey will die pretty much instantly from a well-placed head shot and it will make for a humane kill. Another benefit of headshots is that you will prevent any of the breast meat from being damaged because as long as the shot is accurate no BBs will end up in the breast. Another benefit of the head shot is that it eliminates a chase to find the turkey or a chance that you will never find it after it being wounded and running away. There is pretty much no way that when you make a clean shot at a turkeys head that the turkey is going to be able to run away.

However, a head shot can be difficult because the heads on turkeys are not a large target and they move their heads around often and quickly. This means if you are a less experienced shooter this might not be the best option for you as it will take a good amount of accuracy to make a shot on a smaller portion of the turkey. Also, the further away the turkey is the harder it will be to hit the smaller area of the head compared to a larger area on the body. One last downside is that with a head shot a turkey could move its head at the last moment and you could completely miss the turkey if it ducks its head.

Neck

Another effective area to try and shoot the turkey is going to be in the neck, particularly towards the base of the neck. The primary reason why this can be a good place to aim is that it is a larger area to shoot so even if your shot is off just slightly you are still likely to hit the turkey. Additionally, the vital organs of the turkey are near this area so even with a shot that is slightly off target the chances are you will still hit the bird and be able to kill it. In comparison to movement of the head it takes a turkey more time to move their entire body.

So even if the turkey begins to move right as you are shooting you will still be likely to put a few BBs on the bird with a neck shot.

The biggest downside of a shot placed in the neck area is a potential of damage that it can cause to the meat of the turkey. The majority of the meat on turkeys is on the breasts so if you do have a shot that is off target you risk damaging a large amount of the edible portion of the turkey. Also, since an off target shot might hit non-vital areas of the turkey it could create a chance that you wound the turkey and it gets away or at minimum causes you to chase it down to find it.

Improving Shot Accuracy

One of the best ways to drastically improve your shooting accuracy is to have a stable surface to rest against when you shoot. I discussed a shooting stick earlier and highly recommend it if you are hunting with a shotgun. This will help keep your gun from swaying back and forth which will create inaccurate shots. As I mentioned there are times where you have to wait a while for the turkey to get into a good shooting position so you may end up having to hold your gun up for a long period of time. It is surprising how difficult it is to hold your gun still with nothing to rest it on.

How to take better shots:

- Use a shooting stick
- Lean against the side of a tree
- Kneel down and rest your elbow on your knee
- Take a deep breath just before you shoot

All of the above methods are excellent ways to take more accurate shots with the preference of being the utilization of using a shooting stick which I previously discussed. However, if you do not own a shooting stick or it is just not practical for you to bring one with these other options could be effective for you. If you are hunting in the woods you should not have much difficulty finding a nearby tree to lean against as you shoot. Kneeling is a good option if there is not another tree nearby that is convenient to lean against. Finally, to stabilize your shot you want to take a deep breath just before you shoot. Breathing causes the gun to move up and down. As you get into shooting position and are just about ready to take your shot, take a deep breath. Then aim and slowly let your breath out as you pull the trigger. You should find that this technique greatly improves the accuracy of your shots.

Learn From Missed Shots

Most turkey hunters have missed at least one shot at a turkey. It is important not to get down on yourself when you miss. Turkeys are leery and are not the easiest animal to shoot so it is ok when you miss shots at turkeys. Use missed shots as an opportunity to learn from your mistakes. Try to evaluate what you did well and what you could have done differently. Did you use something to brace yourself for an accurate shot? Did you allow the turkey to get into a clear opening if possible? Did you shoot too soon? These are all questions to ask yourself in order to improve your shooting success.

Now let's look at some what to do after you shoot a turkey...

Step 20: You Shot a Turkey, What's Next?

After Shooting a Turkey, It is Time to Retrieve You Bird

After you shoot a turkey you will want to retrieve your game. Use these tips to successfully collect your game.

Tips after shooting:

- Wait a few minutes
- Pick out a marker where you shot the turkey
- Walk slowly to the turkey
- Check to make sure the turkey is dead before you grab it
- Carrying your bird

Wait a few minutes

Once you shoot a turkey it is normal to be excited and want head out and collect your harvest right away. However, you should wait about 5 minutes before heading out to grab your turkey. First you want to make sure that the turkey is dead so giving it a few minutes to stop moving can be a good idea. If you head out right away and the turkey is still alive it is possible that it will run off and go to a spot where you are unable to retrieve it. However, if you leave it sit for a few minutes it will likely just stay put and die where near where it was shot and will be much easier to find.

The other reason to wait a few minutes before heading out is that there is a chance that there is another turkey in the area that you can shoot. Sounds of a gun going off may not necessarily scare off all of the nearby turkeys so if they heard your calls or they are heading out to your decoy there is still a chance that more turkeys will still come out of hiding. If you head out to soon you ruin any chance you would have had at bagging more than one turkey at the moment. Of course this is only a consideration if the area you hunt allows you to shoot more than one turkey or if you are hunting with a buddy.

Pick out a Marker

As soon as you shoot a turkey you want to look for any markings near where the turkey was after being shot. Sometimes when you shoot the turkey it will drop right in the spot it was shot and should be relatively easy to find. However, there are also times when you shoot a turkey that it may run for a bit before falling over dead. Particularly in those cases where the turkey moved a bit after being shot it is very important to pay attention to where it stopped and take a mental marker.

For example, pick out a tree, rock or pile of dirt in the area that you can use as a location marker to walk to. This makes it much easier to find your turkey. The interesting thing is that when you shoot at something a distance away it is odd how hard it can be to find that spot when you start walking to it. The terrain can just look different and your depth perception can be thrown off. Also, your excitement of shooting a turkey can sometimes make you forget exactly where the turkey was shot. When you have a marker such as a large rock near where you shot it you can easily walk to the rock and then locate your turkey.

Walk Slowly to the Turkey

While you walk to the spot where you think the turkey stopped, it is important to proceed slowly. Sometimes you may have just wounded the turkey so you want to keep an eye on the ground and any brush or grass and look for movement. On the off chance the turkey is still alive and moving it may be necessary to shoot it again.

The other reason you want to walk slowly to the turkey is to look for any other turkeys in the immediate area. It is not uncommon for more than one turkey to be in the same area so there could be others that you could also shoot. Bagging more than one turkey at one time is very satisfying.

Check to Ensure the Turkey is Dead Before You Grab It

Before you pick up a turkey, it is very important to ensure that the turkey is dead. You will first want to stop several feet away and see if you can observe any movement with the turkey. I recommend standing there with your gun ready in case you do happen to see movement you are in a position to take a quick shot if necessary. After observing the turkey for a few minutes without any movement then it is time to check if the turkey is dead at a closer distance. An easy way to do this is by grabbing a stick that is on the ground and poking the turkey to see if it moves. The majority of the time it will be dead but if the turkey shows any movement at all you need to quickly finish off the turkey.

To do this, take a step or two back and make an accurate shot at the head. A head shot at this close of range should kill the turkey instantly. Be aware that if you do need to shoot the turkey again at a close range a shot to the body will likely do a fair amount of damage to the pelt of the animal so if you were planning on keeping the pelt you really should try and shoot it in the head. Additionally, you need to be aware of safety with this situation because you do not want to shoot at something close to you and accidentally hit a rock or something and have the bullet ricochet back at you.

Carrying Your Bird

This might seem obvious to some but there are few different ways that you could carry your turkey out of the field. One of the simplest ways is to grab the turkey by its legs tightly and throw it over your shoulders. Another way is to buy turkey carrying straps which loop around the turkeys legs and sometimes the head and then it provides an easy way to hold the turkey.

Now it's time prepare and preserve the turkey...

Step 21: Turkey Cleaning, Preparation & Preservation

Success! You Shot a Turkey, Now What?

Now that you have shot and retrieved your turkey it is time to get it ready for eating as well as preserving your memories by keeping what you need to make a turkey mount.

What to do with your turkey after bagging it:

- Score your turkey
- Pull off the beard
- Cut off the fan
- Remove the meat

Score the Turkey

Before you start cutting up your turkey or doing anything else to the bird the first thing you want do is to score your turkey. The National Wild Turkey Federation has a scoring system in place for turkeys and based on various factors a turkey will receive an overall score. This score can then be used to compare your bird to other birds and even see if you have harvested a record sized turkey.

Turkey Hunting Made Simple: A Beginners Resource to Turkey Hunting

The components that go into the score of a turkey are its beard length, its weight, the length of its spurs. To get the overall score I have put together a detailed chart below for you to be able to calculate the score. It may seem a little confusing but if you follow the steps you will be able to easily calculate the score in just a few minutes. Also, please see that there is a table of calculations after the chart. You will need to use those tables to give you the correct numbers to input on the scoring chart.

Please note that there several phone apps that calculate the score of a turkey which can save you some time and calculations. Simply search "turkey score calculator" in the app store and you are sure to find at least one turkey scoring app.

Turkey Hunting Made Simple: A Beginners Resource to Turkey Hunting

	Value	Score
Weight		
Pounds	Enter the number of pounds your turkey is (example if the bird is 16 pounds 5 ounces, enter 16)	Example: 16
Ounces	Enter the value from Table 1 that matches up to the amount of ounces the bird is. (Example if the bird is 16 pounds 5 ounces you can see that 5 on the table equals 0.3125) so your value is 0.3125	Example: 0.3125
	Weight Score(Add up the pounds and ounces values)	16 + 0.3125 = **16.3125**
Beard		
Inches	Enter the length of the beard in inches, whole inches only (example if the beard is 6 and 3/16 of an inch enter 6)	Example: 6
Fraction of Inch	Enter the value from table 2 that lines up with the fractions of an inch the beard is (example if the beard is 6 and 13/16 of an inch enter the value lines up with .8125)	Example: .8125
	Beard Score(Add the inches score and the fractions of an inch value, then multiply the value times 2)	Example: 6 + .8125= 6.8125 x 2 = **13.625**
Spurs		
Left Spur Inches	Enter the length of the left in inches, whole inches only (example if the beard is 5 and 14/16 of an inch enter 5)	Example: 5
Left Spur Fraction of Inch	Enter the value from table 2 that lines up with the fractions of an inch the left spur is is (example if the left spur is 5 and 14/16 of an inch enter the value that lines up with 14/16 which is .875)	Example: .875
Right Spur Inches	Enter the length of the right spur in inches, whole inches only (example if the right spur is 7 and 15/16 of an inch enter 7)	Example: 7
Right Spur Fraction of Inch	Enter the value from table 2 that lines up with the fractions of an inch the right spur is is (example if the right spur is 7 and 15/16 of an inch enter the value that lines up with 15/16 which is .9375)	Example: .9375
	Spur Score (Add each of the 4 scores together, then multiply their value times 10	Example: 5+.875+7+.9375= 13.8125 then multiply by 10 = **138.125**
	Total Score (Add the total weight score plus the total beard score plus the total spur score)	Example: 16.3125 + 13.625 + 138.125 = **163.938**

Table 1			Table 2	
User Selection	Value		User Selection	Value
0	0		0/16	0
1	0.0625		1/16	0.0625
2	0.125		2/16 (1/8)	0.125
3	0.1875		3/16	0.1875
4	0.25		4/16 (1/4)	0.25
5	0.3125		5/16	0.3125
6	0.375		6/16 (3/8)	0.375
7	0.4375		7/16	0.4375
8	0.5		8/16 (1/2)	0.5
9	0.5625		9/16	0.5625
10	0.625		10/16 (5/8)	0.625
11	0.6875		11/16	0.6875
12	0.75		12/16 (3/4)	0.75
13	0.8125		13/16	0.8125
14	0.875		14/16 (7/8)	0.875
15	0.9375		15/16	0.9375

Pull off the Beard

Now that you have calculated the score of your turkey it is time to remove the beard. This is a very easy task because all you need to do is grab the beard close to where it is attached to the body of the turkey and pull. As long as you get a tight grip and pull hard the beard should come off with ease. After you have the beard removed you will want to put some Borax on the base of the beard where it was pulled off from the turkey. Borax is a preserving chemical powder that you can buy at pretty much any large retail stores such as Wal-Mart or Target.

Cut Off the Fan

One of the largest prizes from shooting a turkey is its fan. Basically the fan is the large tail feathers on the back of the turkey and the secondary tail feathers which are the smaller ring of feathers at the base of the large fan feathers. To remove the fan you simply grab the fan feathers and hold them tightly together in your hand. Then take your hunting knife and cut off the fan by following around the base of the fan, ensuring that you do not cut too close to the feathers as to not risk the tail feathers separating. Place the fan into a large plastic bag and store it in a refrigerator until you are ready to create your turkey mount.

Cut Off the Spurs

Another part of the turkey that people often like to keep as a prize are the spurs. Again the spurs are the claws of a tom or jake turkey that are located on the back of the legs. You could use a hack saw or band saw to cut them off easily. One tip to make the process a little easier is to freeze the legs before you attempt to cut the spurs off. This makes the entire leg stiffer so it allows for easier cutting because the leg will be hard rather than soft so it will stay in shape while cutting. After removing the spurs some people simply place them in a cup of salt for a few weeks and allow to dry them out. Once dried then they drill a hole through a base to make a necklace or bracelet.

Creating a Trophy Turkey Mount

Combining the beard, fan and even spurs into a mounted plaque is a great way to remember your successful hunt and show off your turkey to friends and family. To create this plaque you could either elect to bring in the parts to a local taxidermist or you could do the mounting yourself. A taxidermist might charge somewhere around $80 - $200 or so to create a fan mount. Of course this could be more or less based on the taxidermist and the type of material or wood that the plaque is made out of. Depending on your level of comfort trying something like mounting it might be worth the expense. However, if you feel ambitious you could buy a fan mounting kit for around $20 - $40 and do the work yourself. If you do elect to go this route there are several steps do to it successfully and the best thing I recommend you to do in order to learn to make a fan is to do a web search on "how to make a fan turkey mount" and you will find a lot of videos and resources that outline the process.

Remove the Meat

Now that you have removed all of the trophy parts from the turkey it is finally time to remove the meat from the turkey to eat. The great thing about turkeys compared to many other wild game is that the flavor is very similar to what many people are used to which is store bought turkey. Sure there is some noticeable difference between store bought turkey and wild turkey but it is not going to be as much as an unfamiliar flavor such as ducks or geese.

To complete the cleaning process, you will need a hunting knife, disposable gloves (if you desire), water, freezer size Ziploc bags, trash bag(s) (if you will take remains home with you vs. discarding on site), and a cooler with ice. Unless it is very cold out or you will be going right home and live very close to your hunting site, I would recommend that you bring a cooler with you. If you don't plan to clean the turkeys on site you would need the cooler to carry the whole, uncleaned birds. You might even want to have a cooler that you dedicate specifically to this purpose as you probably wouldn't want to use it for anything else afterwards.

Steps to De-Breast your turkey:

You should try to clean the turkey within 1 hour of shooting it to ensure that the meat is still fresh and does not have a chance to go bad before you get it into a cool area. If you are hunting in very cold temperatures you can wait a little longer; however, if you are hunting during the warm early season you should consider cleaning your turkeys shortly after they are shot, or at least putting them in a cooler.

STEP 1: Place the turkey on its back with its breasts facing up towards your face.

STEP 2: Use your knife to cut a small slit into the skin underneath the feathers on the chest. The slit should be large enough to reach two thumbs into.

STEP 3: Place both of your thumbs into the slit and use the rest of your fingers grab ahold of the skin and pull it towards the wings of the turkey to expose the breast. You will do this by pulling your hands in opposite directions to separate the skin. It may take several pulls and you will need to readjust your grip several times, you will also need to pull hard to ensure you separate the skin from the breast meat.

STEP 4: After the skin/feathers are pulled away from the breast, take your knife and use it to cut along one side of the breast bone keeping the knife blade firmly against the breast bone. The breast bone is located in the middle of the breast of the turkey.

STEP 5: With one hand continue using the knife to work the blade along the breast bone plate while using the other hand to gently pull the meat away from bone.

STEP 6: Once you have one breast removed repeat steps 5 & 5 to remove the remaining turkey breast.

STEP 7: Place both of the breasts in a freezer sized Ziploc bags and put them in a cooler.

STEP 8: Dispose of the remaining turkey carcass by bagging them and taking them home for disposal or by leaving them in a spot where they are somewhat hidden from human traffic. They will most likely be taken care of rather quickly by coyotes, hawks or other animals.

STEP 9: When you arrive at home take the breasts out of the Ziploc bags and run them under cold water to wash away any remaining feathers or blood. If there is any remaining fat on the breasts use your fingers to pinch the fat and pull it off the breasts.

STEP 10: If you are eating the meat within the next 24 hours return the breasts to Ziploc bags and refrigerate them or freeze all meat immediately after completing the cleaning process if you will eat the meat at a later date.

Final Words as You Start Turkey Hunting

Congratulations! You have taken your first step in becoming a successful turkey hunter.

Your Success is in Your Hands
If you have made it this far it is clear that you are passionate about turkey hunting and you want to shoot more turkeys. Remember that hunting is fun but also challenging. Regardless of the success you have ensure you take time to enjoy the time you spend outdoors.

Just Get Started
Getting started with anything can be challenging at first. Think back to when you first started tying your shoes. At first it was difficult but after time it became second nature. This can be the same with turkey hunting. The more you do it the better you will get.

Make Progress Every Day
Using the steps learned in this book will help improve your turkey hunting skills. I encourage you to make some type of progress each day of the season. Keep reading books, follow hunting blogs and watch YouTube videos. Six months from now you will be surprised how far you have made it by spending time learning more about turkey hunting each day.

Made in the USA
Monee, IL
11 January 2020